The Arrest

A DRAMA IN TWO ACTS

By Jean Anouilh

Translated By Lucienne Hill

SAMUEL FRENCH, INC.
25 West 45th Street NEW YORK 10036
7623 Sunset Boulevard HOLLYWOOD 90046
LONDON *TORONTO*

PRINTED IN U. S. A.

ISBN 0 573 60565 3

LIST OF CHARACTERS

THE MAN

THE YOUNG MAN

THE SMALL BOY

THE POLICE SUPERINTENDENT

THE NIGHT PORTER

THE HEAD PORTER

MUSICIANS

ALBERTO BACHMANN

THE MOTHER

THE YOUNG WOMAN

THE GRANDMOTHER

THE MAN'S TWO CHILDREN

THE LITTLE GIRL

THE OLD WOMAN } The same
THE GIRL IN THE CATHEDRAL } character

A WAITER, an OLD WOMAN, the CHILDREN in the tea-dance, hotel guests.

The Arrest

ACT ONE

The gloomy lobby of a kind of provincial Grand Hotel, architecturally pretentious. All of it is old, run down, a bit seedy. Shabby gilt and chipped plasterwork and a general air of having seen better days.

One hears the distant strains of a band.

Enter a MAN *of about fifty, followed by a* YOUNG MAN*; both in raincoats. The* YOUNG MAN *carries an overnight bag. The* MAN *stops and looks around, as if troubled.*

MAN. This is the place.

YOUNG MAN. (*Noncommittally.*) Yes. This is it.

MAN. There's nobody here, but this is the place. The evening concert is still on. I can hear the orchestra playing on the bandstand outside. (*He listens.*) They're still playing the same silly music. Odd that the Casino should still be open at the beginning of October. They must have extended the season. The colonial visitors—there were a lot of those in the old days—always preferred these last few weeks of summer. I don't know if things have changed since we lost our colonies . . . (*He wanders about a bit and stops suddenly before a big, heavily gilded mirror. He murmurs, looking at himself.*) What a face . . . After forty, all mirrors are alarming, especially those you saw yourself in when young. I spent a great many summers here as a child. (*He turns to the* YOUNG MAN *who has hung back a little, his travelling bag at his feet.*) It was very good of you to let me share your taxi. There wouldn't have been another at this time of night—not at that little country station.

YOUNG MAN. (*Noncommittally.*) No trouble. I was coming here anyway.

MAN. Stupid my car breaking down like that. And as I was so near this little resort, I thought I might as well spend two days here while they do the repairs. (*He explains.*) They have to send away to Paris for spare parts. You always break down in the country and the spares are always in town, have you noticed? My one hope was a milk train with a three hour wait on a cold station or the only taxi. And you were in it. It was very kind of you.

YOUNG MAN. (*Neutrally.*) Don't mention it. I told you. I was coming here anyway.

MAN. A belated cure? Have you come to take the waters, like my worthy colonial friends in the old days?

YOUNG MAN. (*Uncommunicatively.*) My wife is here with my small daughter.

MAN. (*Exclaiming as he looks round.*) Lord, it's a good thirty years since I set foot in this place. I was a young man when I saw it last, but my childhood impressions are what stayed with me. It was all vaster and more luxurious in my memory. In actual fact it's rather seedy and a lot smaller than I thought.

YOUNG MAN. (*Noncommittally.*) A classic reaction. A matter of scale, no doubt.

MAN. Or imagination . . . Scientists have done some very serious studies in an attempt to explain what the world might look like through the thousand facetted eyes of a fly! They've never thought to use this admirable scientific discipline to tell us how the world looks through the eyes of a child. Science has a tendency to prefer houseflies.

YOUNG MAN. (*With a smile.*) Just as well, perhaps . . .

MAN. (*Smiling too.*) For the children, yes . . . (*He paces about the vast room, touching things, wonderingly.*) Strange, it's like diving into the sea . . . We forget what we once were and after that we live beside our own children without attempting to know them. We merely try to train them to be us, in miniature. And then, once past the bend in the road, when we have seen for the first time Death's calm face, patiently waiting, we suddenly start to look at them attentively. You'll see. (*He looks at him and smiles.*) You'll have to wait a good long while yet . . . Twenty five, twenty six years.

YOUNG MAN. Twenty seven.

MAN. At your age, children are still balky and assertive little enemies. And then, thirty years later, we look at them. Too late, usually. It's other people's children we look at . . . And we begin, at the same time, to look at the world through their eyes. They are our masters. Only they know what's important still. They could teach us everything if we would only listen. (*He murmurs.*) Too late. (*He adds strangely.*) Heaven knows I haven't had much contact with them, with the life I've led. But now, if circumstances forced me to choose an ordinary trade, I think I'd be a schoolmaster. (*He adds with a smile.*) In tiny little schools, of course, because teachers very quickly turn into idiots and monsters, like the rest . . . (*Enter the* NIGHT PORTER, *dragging his slippers.*) Ah, here's someone at last. The haunted castle isn't quite asleep.

I might possibly get myself a room. (*He goes to the* MAN.) Could you let me have a room for a night or two? I'm in transit . . .

PORTER. (*Looking at his board.*) Certainly, sir. Bone empty we are, at this time of year. I can give you number twenty seven. Lovely room with twin beds and big bathroom—a bit ancient of course, like everything else here—a bit gloomy, but very spacious . . .

MAN. (*With a smile.*) I know. I've known all your rooms . . .

PORTER. Ah, well, if you know the establishment, sir . . . Number 27 looks out on to the grounds, just above the bandstand. You can listen to the band of an evening, sir, before you go to sleep, if you care for that sort of thing.

MAN. That's exactly what I need.

PORTER. (*Unhooking the massive key.*) Follow me, sir, if you would. Any luggage, sir?

MAN. No.

PORTER. You can register tomorrow, sir. There's nobody in reception. There's no hurry, I don't suppose.

MAN. No. (*They go out along the big dark corridor. The* MAN *asks as he goes.*) Is that the band playing outside?

PORTER. No, sir. The band went off duty an hour ago. They've all gone home. That's my radio. It keeps me awake. You tend to nod off if you work nights . . . (*They go out into the darkness. The* YOUNG MAN *has not moved. The radio music stops. An* ANNOUNCER *comes on the air.*)

ANNOUNCER. Here is a news flash. Frederick Walter, the so called 'Invisible Man'—whose real face nobody has ever seen and who carried out his seventeenth hold-up at a bank in Lyons today, was intercepted by the police this evening. After a short gun battle, in which two officers were seriously wounded, Walter made his getaway in a hijacked car, taking the driver with him as a hostage. Road blocks have been set up on all main roads. We have just heard that the driver of the stolen vehicle has been found unhurt in a wood some twenty miles from the scene of the crime. The 'Invisible Man' is still at large.

(A YOUNG WOMAN *has come in, in nightclothes, her hair hanging loose. The* YOUNG MAN *switches off the radio.*)

YOUNG WOMAN. You're back?

YOUNG MAN. Yes.

YOUNG WOMAN. And you'll be off tomorrow, after you've hurt us both again?

YOUNG MAN. I had to see you.

YOUNG WOMAN. Look at me. Not pretty your wife, is she? I hate tears too. They make you ugly.

YOUNG MAN. (*Dully.*) I'd like to go up to our room.

YOUNG WOMAN. I think you'd better book one for yourself.

YOUNG MAN. (*Dully again.*) I'd like to go up to our room.

YOUNG WOMAN. To get me to comfort you for leaving us? (*He does not answer. She smiles a wan smile, pushes her hair back and leads the way along the corridor. He picks up his suitcase and follows her silently. The stage is empty for a moment, then the members of the band come in, after their evening stroll. They are a vulgar lot, noisy and loudly dressed. At first they all talk at once, so that one doesn't quite know who has said what. They are dressed in the fashion of the Twenties.*)

MUSICIANS.

I feel better after that little walk. Lovely grounds they have here I must say.

Oh very lively it was! Great night life they have here! One drunk, two policemen on bicycles and two dogs. At it like knives—the dogs I mean.

Great fun it was cheering them on. Do you think they like that sort of thing—being watched I mean?

Shouldn't be surprised. You get dog perverts just as you do men.

Oh stop it. You've got it on the brain!

Oh listen to her! Hot as mustard you are and so's she! Can't get enough of it, the pair of you.

In this hole? You're not joking. When I think of that season we did at the Casino in Dieppe! One long whirl that was!

You take what you can in this job.

Symphonic music is on the way out anyway. It's all ragtime these days. We'll have to turn our hands to it like everybody else.

Never!

And that's what we beat the Boche for! The Americans have taken over everything.

(*One of them sprawls in an armchair and takes his shoes off, as he sings:*)

It's a long way to Tipp—

MUSICIAN. (*Exasperated.*) The English sang that, you fool!

GIRL. I don't care what you say, the Americans were a fine bunch of boys! And generous with it. Chocolate bars, chewing gum, cigarettes! I did a season in a great big rest camp early in 1918, down near Biarritz. Pots of money they had. The girls in the orchestra were crazy about them—

OLD MUSICIAN. Nice goings on there were, I bet.

GIRL. What do you expect? Five women and five hundred soldiers—you can't fight Nature!

VOICE. (*Singing.*)

Love
Keeps the heart a burning
Love
Keeps the world a turning

GIRL. There was a girl—big gawky thing, played the alto fiddle—she fell for a baby and got the fellow to marry her! We all went to the wedding. The gilt wore off when she got him back home though. He turned out to be a docker.

VOICE.

Deceptive thing a uniform.
Treacherous, lecherous, marvellous love . . .

OMNES. Come on, boys and girls, Beauty sleep time!

GIRL. It's getting cooler now, but in August! —the heat up in those rooms! And I slept in the raw!

MUSICIAN. Accommodation at the Casino! Sounds very grand, but they don't tell you it's in the maids' rooms! Wouldn't be so bad if the maids were thrown in. Not on your life—they're all living out. There's nothing drearier than a maid's room—without a maid! (*He guffaws at this.*)

GIRL. (*Going out, with her arm round her friend's waist.*) Dirty old devil! That's all you two ever think about!

OLD MUSICIAN. (*To the* OTHER MAN.) How about a

hand of poker. Up in my room? I've got a nip of brandy.

MUSICIAN. Right. Ten francs a hundred though, no more!

GIRL. Oh you and your cards!

MUSICIAN. Got to do something! We're too old for women!

ONE LAST VOICE. (*As they go upstairs.*) I think I'll wash my feet tonight . . . (*They all go up. A* YOUNG WOMAN, THE MOTHER, *has remained behind, together with* ALBERTO, *who sits glowering in an armchair.*)

MOTHER. Aren't you coming up?

ALBERTO. Not yet, do you mind? I'm having a smoke.

MOTHER. I must see if he's asleep.

ALBERTO. (*Irritably.*) You're such a bore with that brat of yours!

MOTHER. You know he can't get to sleep until he knows I'm back. He's very highly strung . . .

ALBERTO. Rubbish, you make a point of waking him up. And while you're cuddling the little darling and getting him off to sleep again I'm kicking my heels in my room, aren't I?

MOTHER. I've got to be so careful with him, you know that. He's odd enough as it is . . . He suspects something. Ah, now don't sulk, my fat ram! (*She gives him a little stroke on the head. He shies away.*)

ALBERTO. What you don't seem to realise is, your fat ram will get sick of it one of these days.

MOTHER. (*Wildly.*) Alberto, my great bear!

ALBERTO. A jealous husband, right! —that's one thing. You buy him a drink, you listen to his tale of woe, you pat him on the back. At least you know where you are. But a jealous little whippet like that one! —spying on you every minute of the day!

MOTHER. I think that's very sweet, him being jealous of his mother!

ALBERTO. So touching it's making me weep! Go up to your brat then! go on!

MOTHER. If you had a child of your own! . . .

ALBERTO. Don't tempt the devil. Get upstairs, go on. (*He takes off his shoes, loosens his collar and sprawls back.*) Lovely idea, these little evening walks but my feet are in a mush.

MOTHER. (*Sidling over, tenderly.*) It was nice tonight, though, wasn't it, in that little summerhouse on our own? (*She strokes his neck shyly.*) Do you remember the night you took me on the grass, behind the shrubbery, while the others were looking at the moonlight up on the little headland? Oh the bliss we had that night!

ALBERTO. So did the others, don't you worry!

MOTHER. What—they didn't see us, did they?

ALBERTO. You make me weep you're so innocent.

MOTHER. Oh, you see evil everywhere! I shan't be long, you great big bull you! The moment he's asleep I'll scratch on your door.

ALBERTO. (*Gloomily.*) Right. (*She starts to go hesitantly, and turns back.*)

MOTHER. I don't like leaving you alone. You aren't planning to meet someone, are you? You're such a devil with women!

ALBERTO. Go on up I said! Who do you expect me to meet out of season, in this hole? There's nobody here now under ninety.

MOTHER. (*Flinging herself onto him and kissing him greedily.*) My great big wolf! It's crazy the way you get under my skin, you!

(*The* MAN *has come down. He stiffens, unaccountably,*

at seeing them embraced. She senses his presence, utters a little cry and runs off.)

MAN. (*Just before she goes.*) I'm so sorry. (*He looks at* ALBERTO *for a second, with a touch of hostility. Then he says:*) Excuse me. Is the bar closed?

ALBERTO. After eleven o'clock everything's closed here. What a dump. Good for infections of the lower bowel though, it seems. Taking the waters, are you?

MAN. No. Just passing through.

ALBERTO. Take my advice then, pass through quick! You'll go mad here.

MAN. Are you under treatment yourself?

ALBERTO. Yes, but not for my inside. For another chronic ailment; work! I'm in the band. Here for the season. It's nearly over, thank God—only another fortnight. Mind you, if I hadn't got myself a winter season on the coast, I'd be out of work. There are fewer and fewer cafe orchestras in Paris now. (*He gets to his feet suddenly, very much man of the world, and makes to introduce himself.*) So sorry—my name's Bachmann—Alberto Bachmann . . . (*He waits for the* MAN *to give his own name. The* MAN *says nothing.* ALBERTO *goes on.*) If we can find some glasses, I've got a flask of brandy. Always carry it. Good for colds, you know. Let's have a nip or two, shall we? Such a bore having to go to bed!

MAN. Yes, why not? (*He remains alone for a moment while the other man goes out for the glasses. The* MAN *picks up the* MOTHER'S *scarf and smells it furtively.* ALBERTO *comes back.*)

ALBERTO. (*Seeing him with the scarf.*) That's my bird's. She forgot to take it up. Women forget everything. I had a girl once who forgot her knickers in the taxi. When I came to pay I saw them on the seat and stuffed them in my pocket. I ran in—I was late for the five o'clock show. In Ostend it was. We were playing up on a bandstand, with the audience all round us. Big fat Belgians, all very proper. It was August and I was streaming—I always sweat a lot when I'm playing. Very emotional piece it was, with the soprano giving her all. I go to wipe my face with my handkerchief and pull out the knickers. (*He sniggers.*) I thought the band would split their sides! And the audience picked it up, of course. And the singer screeching away, oblivious! We near on got the sack, all of us. All for a woman leaving her smalls about. Irresponsible lot! Here's to you!

MAN. And you. It's an easy life though, yours, isn't it?

ALBERTO. I must be honest, it's not like going down a mine. Between shows we're free enough— We're holiday makers too, in a sense. And as for women, plenty of openings there—if you'll pardon the phrase! If the ladies get bored on holiday who do they turn to? —the boys in the band! Mark you, as we're all more or less teamed up with the girls in the band from the start it makes the fur fly a bit. By the end of the season nobody's speaking to anybody! It's lucky if you don't come to blows. Then you join another group and you start all over again. That's life!

MAN. And music?

ALBERTO. As a youngster you aim for the stars—don't we all? Every one a little Rubenstein, planning his concert tour. And then, well, you grub for a living. And you sleep around. And you spend all you earn keeping up a front—well, you have to, in these resorts, when you mix with the customers . . . You get drunk now and then, you play cards with the boys . . . Life goes on . . . Do other people do any better?

MAN. (*Strangely.*) And love—what about that?

ALBERTO. (*Sniggering.*) Know about love, do you?

MAN. I was a little indiscreet earlier on. I overheard the end of your conversation. She has a child, I gather. She's married, is she?

ALBERTO. Yes. She works the odd season to make up the money. Her husband doesn't earn much. She learnt the piano as a girl, won the odd prize. Then, during the war, when he was away at the front, she took it up professionally. After the Armistice she carried on with it. You get used to independence. And it gets her little treasure out into the fresh air—he's a bit bronchial, so it's off to the seaside every summer. But don't talk to me about married women! They're the worst! Good pair of thighs, easy to talk to and lively in bed—and before you know where you are there's the brat on your hands, and you have to play Father! Well, as little as possible in my case! Another two weeks and I'm off. I'm doing a winter season in Menton.

MAN. And what about her?

ALBERTO. (*Cheerfully.*) Back to Paris with the old man. And the brat's at school, thank God.

MAN. (*Eyeing him strangely.*) Does the boy resent you?

ALBERTO. Yes. Green with jealousy he is. Ears and eyes wide open, sniffing the wind. You'll see him tomorrow I should think. Eyes as big as saucers, staring at you and not a word . . . I keep telling myself he's only a child, but he makes me squirm sometimes . . . (*He stops, embarrassed.*) Why am I telling you all this? . . .

MAN. You have to talk to someone . . .

ALBERTO. (*Shifting under his gaze.*) Another little drop?

MAN. (*Refusing with a smile.*) No, thank you.

ALBERTO. You're right. Your tongue's like lead in the morning. (*He puts his flask away in his pocket and gets to his feet.*) Bedtime! That's the trouble with this job, too much lifting the elbow. Working in an office or a factory you don't get the temptations. Right, I'm off upstairs. The kid will be asleep. She makes out he lies awake every night, sniffing her scent on the pillow, until she comes in. I ask you! Complicate everything—that's women! After that she slips out in her shift and curls up with me.

MAN. Does he ever wake up?

ALBERTO. Yes, once he did. He looked for her everywhere. He came right to our door. We could hear him breathing outside. And then he went back to bed. She'd told him she was going to the lavatory. For two nights after that, she didn't dare move. Talk about involved! All for a brat! Nothing's straightforward with women. Ciao then. See you tomorrow, we might have a drink if you're still here?

MAN. Yes, indeed. I expect to stay for a while.

(ALBERTO *has gone, carrying his shoes. The* MAN *remains alone, and motionless. The old* NIGHT PORTER *crosses the stage in his slippers, doing his rounds. He switches off a few lights. The* MAN *settles in an armchair in the half light. Suddenly he sits up. The* YOUNG WOMAN *tears wildly through the hall, in her nightdress, and runs out into the grounds. A moment later, the* YOUNG MAN *appears, half dressed, and sets off in pursuit. One hears him shouting 'Anne Marie! Anne Marie!' The* MAN *listens, tense. Cries are heard: 'Leave me alone! You brute! Let me go! You're hurting me!' The* YOUNG MAN *appears, carrying the* Young Woman *who is struggling between sobs, and scratching his face. Exhausted he flings her down into the armchair, where she crouches, glaring up at him wildly.*)

Young Woman. Let me be! Let me be! I want to die!

Young Man. Yes and what about the child?

Young Woman. You've deserted her already, haven't you? My mother will have her. She'll be very happy there. Happier than with us.

Young Man. (*After an anguished pause.*) You can't stay here in your nightdress, in the middle of the night. Let's go back to our room.

Young Woman. What for? We'll only quarrel and she'll wake up and start to cry. Let her sleep in peace, at least.

Young Man. Can't we try not to quarrel any more? Let's just lie down and try to sleep.

Young Woman. You know we won't be able to. Why did you come back?

Young Man. I couldn't leave you on your own.

Young Woman. And you can't leave your fancy woman either, can you? You've made a real mess of it all, my poor lad, considering how you hate tears.

Young Man. (*Heavily.*) Give me a year. Give me a few months. I'll come back.

Young Woman. You're in love with her.

Young Man. (*Dully.*) I'm not. You're the one I love.

Young Woman. You want her then, put it that way. It's the same thing to me.

Young Man. I've been unfaithful to you before, with odd girls I met, and I never told you. It made no difference. Women never understand. They put everything on the same level. I used to come back to you both and that was home and country to me. (*A long pause. They stand silent and motionless, facing each other. Then the* YOUNG WOMAN *begins to speak, in a strange, quiet little voice.*)

YOUNG WOMAN. I don't know what made me want to drown myself—the water is so cold and black at night—besides I can swim. I don't know why I wanted to die. I'm already dead. (*A short pause and she goes on in the same small voice.*) It's all quite simple, really. I was a provincial girl who felt a little submerged by her family. I ran away with you, you got me with child and you married me. You gave me two years of happiness and then I died . . . Lives are like that . . . I shall go home to my mother, to her lovely house in the main square, where the wardrobes smell good, and I'll serve tea to her friends in the big green drawing room, as nicely as I always did. I don't suppose they'll even notice that I'm dead. I'll listen to their smiling comments—and, mixed with the slight contempt for my bad marriage, there'll be a hint of pity now, because I've been left. 'Didn't we say so! It was only a matter of time! A girl from one of the best families in town! Who could have married the heir to the Delachaume Chemical Industries—all she had to do was lift her little finger.' And you don't get divorced where I come from. I shall start my life again as a dead thing, that's all. I might even come back here one summer—later, much later, to remind myself, with Mother and the children. (*She adds lightly.*) I didn't tell you—you've had enough on your mind, my poor love—but I'm expecting another. (*She adds crisply.*) It will be simpler for that one. He won't pine for you like our little girl. We won't ever mention you to him. You see, I'm quite calm. I shall go up now. I shall lie on my back, thinking of nothing, and stare at the dark. It's full of pictures, the dark. When you come up, try not to wake her . . . (*She goes out silently. The* YOUNG MAN *has not moved. The* MAN *murmurs, in the darkness.*)

MAN. I know it's none of my business, but . . .

YOUNG MAN. (*Starting.*) Were you there?

MAN. Yes, I'm sorry. I couldn't help listening. (*He adds softly.*) Don't do it.

YOUNG MAN. (*Like a sleepwalker.*) I'm in love with a girl who's probably a whore. But I didn't know what love was before.

MAN. (*Quietly.*) Don't do it. It never works.

YOUNG MAN. (*As if to himself.*) It had got so that I couldn't breathe . . . This contented little existence . . . that couldn't be life for me.

MAN. (*Quietly.*) Yes. It could.

YOUNG MAN. Affection seeps through you like glue. It leaves you slimy.

MAN. (*Shortly.*) Yes. And without it, afterwards you slowly die.

YOUNG MAN. (*Violently.*) I'll pay then! I'll pay for everything!

MAN. (*Quietly.*) Very dearly. And you won't be the only one who does. I know advice means nothing. Past fifty, we're all old gangsters; we've done all there is to do and we're wanted by all the police forces in the world. There isn't even enough time ahead to serve all the prison sentences we deserve, if we get caught. And we don't care. But the tears of one innocent child, tears that we didn't even see at the time—those we do care about, in some strange way. And that's why one dies so badly.

YOUNG MAN. (*Hard.*) I've time for that.

MAN. It goes very fast.

YOUNG MAN. (*Looks at him and shouts.*) Look, I don't know you!

MAN. No. We just met at the station.

(*The* YOUNG MAN *gives him another look and goes swiftly out. The old* NIGHT PORTER *has come back with his lamp. He notices the* MAN *who doesn't appear to have moved.*)

PORTER. Still here, sir? What are you doing, sir? —dreaming?

MAN. I'm not sleepy.

PORTER. Our colonial visitors in the old days—they didn't sleep too well either . . . There was always one or other to chat with late at night . . . I got to know some interesting folk in those days, men with important positions in Madagascar or Algeria . . . That's all over now! The Casino Hotel has nobody of that quality these days. Stands to reason, with your Social Security, your poor man takes the waters too. . . . Mark you, mineral water did nothing for the rich anyway. So for the poor, with their real illnesses —well, I ask you! Ah, well, that's progress! No, I'm talking about the days just after the first world war, when there was still a resident orchestra at the Casino. We had one of sorts right up to Munich really . . . Oh those musicians! Rum bunch of jokers that lot! What a racket at nights . . . Especially up on their floor! We put them up on the sixth floor, in the maids' rooms . . . There were some to-ings and fro-ings in the passages after midnight I can tell you! The guests of course, were less given to that sort of thing—too careful of their precious little health. Although there's some I've known . . . colonials in fact . . . Used to having women when they fancied it out there I suppose . . . And then, after a bit of scuttling in nightshirts everybody settled down to go to sleep—and the night porter could have himself his own little bit of fun, on the quiet. We make a great todo about our little urges, but they don't amount to much, for most of us! Besides, sleep's good too . . . like a little death . . . You forget everything. One last creaking door, one last randy customer creeping back to his own cool little bed—glad to be going to sleepybies alone, like when he was little. And the night grows quiet again, like a big drowsy animal . . . Just one deep sigh, as it turns over . . . The night's a living thing too, you know . . . but only the night porter knows that—or a guest like you sometimes, waiting for the anguish to wear off . . . (*He adds mysteriously.*) Some funny things go on, sir, at night . . . At that time, round about three o'clock—I'm talking about those years after the first world war, when we still had musicians living in—I used to hear something creeping about, like a mouse . . . It was a little lad, the son of the woman pianist we had here. He used to sleepwalk a bit. Something wasn't going quite right for him. He used to appear in his nightshirt and go to the big French windows that looked out onto the grounds—I always left them wide open on summer nights. He'd look out into the darkness for a bit and then he'd go and curl up in an armchair. Bit of a quirk that, really. I didn't dare say anything to him. I've heard tell you mustn't disturb sleepwalkers or they might hurt themselves . . . Unhappy little fellow that one . . . His mother wasn't a bad sort. She looked after him well, and she cared about him. Clean little white socks always and nicely ironed shirts. But she was a bit loose, you might say. And that knocked him off his feet, really . . . I read an article in a medical paper somebody left here once—it seems that sort of thing upsets children and they carry it about for the rest of their lives . . . I wonder what became of him when he grew up? I don't suppose we'll ever know . . . Ah well, we all have our cross to bear . . . If it isn't that it's another thing . . . I wasn't all that happy myself as a youngster . . . (*He goes waffling on.*) Although they do say . . . And then, as time wears on . . . (*His voice slowly dies. Silence. And then the sound of his steady breathing. He is asleep. The* MAN *sits with his eyes open in the dark. After a while a little sound is heard. A small white figure appears at the end of the passage. It is a little* BOY *of about ten, in a long white nightshirt. He goes to the French windows, looks out into the darkness for a while and then curls up in an armchair with a sigh and soon drops off to sleep. After a while the* MAN *goes to him, covers him with his raincoat and squats down by his chair, watching him as he sleeps. Now only the* NIGHT PORTER'S *breathing is heard. The lights fade slowly to blackout. When they come up again, it is dawn. One faint ray of sun appears outside. The* MAN *has spent the night asleep in a chair. The* NIGHT PORTER *is asleep too, sprawled over his desk. The little* BOY *has gone. But the* MAN'S *raincoat is still on the floor beside the armchair. From the passage, the two* OLD MUSICIANS *absurdly rigged out for fishing, come bouncing in. They look very much alive. One hears the vague crackle of the* NIGHT PORTER'S *radio, which he has left on. After a little music the keep fit class begins, to the accompaniment of jolly music.*)

1ST MUSICIAN. Going fishing?

2ND MUSICIAN. No. I'm going fishing!

1ST MUSICIAN. Oh. I thought you were going fishing! (*They go out, laughing. The* MAN *wakes up. The* NIGHT PORTER *wakes too and sees him.*)

PORTER. Hullo—did you spent the night in that chair, sir?

MAN. Yes, I fell asleep.

PORTER. It's nippy this morning. You can tell it's October. (*He gathers his things together.*) I'm going off duty now. A good strong cup of coffee and then bed. I'll be back at two when the other fellow's done his stint. Anything you need, sir?

MAN. Nothing, thanks. What's that young man doing here—the one with the young wife, who arrived last night?

PORTER. They came in mid September. She was supposed to be taking a cure, so they said. But the young fellow looked as though he knew these parts. He told me once that he'd been here as a child. We chatted about those days but I didn't really remember him. Stands to reason . . . a little nipper twenty years back . . . Besides, he didn't go into it much. He's a bit on the close side. Apart from that, they're a nice young couple. Only, between ourselves, there's sand in the works somewhere. They don't get on too well. He's got a bit of fluff somewhere. He comes and goes. At their age—what a way to carry on! Time enough to cheat and bicker later on, when you start to feel smothered in bed at night! They've got everything those two—love, good health and a lovely little girl . . . It's sad for the child of course, as usual. You help yourself to anything you fancy and you leave the kids to pay the bill! That's life . . . and we won't change it! (*The* HEAD PORTER *has come bustling in. He is a younger man.*)

HEAD PORTER. Good morning, Joseph.

NIGHT PORTER. Morning, Monsieur Leon, sir.

HEAD PORTER. Everything all right?

NIGHT PORTER. All in order, sir.

HEAD PORTER. Goodnight, then.

NIGHT PORTER. Goodnight, sir, and a lovely sunny morning it is, too! (*He goes out. The keep fit class is heard faintly on the radio.*)

HEAD PORTER. You arrived last night, sir?

MAN. Yes.

HEAD PORTER. Would you like breakfast down here, sir? The kitchen's open at seven fifteen . . . I can't seem to find your registration slip, sir. My colleague must have omitted to ask you to fill one up . . . If you would be so kind, sir? It's only a formality, but the police are very strict in this little locality, although nothing ever happens here. Perhaps because nothing ever happens . . . they'll be along to collect the registrations at eight.

(*The* MAN *gets up nonchalantly and starts to fill up the form. The radio crackles. The music has stopped. A voice announces: 'And now, here is Philippe Fessard with the news. Over to you, Philippe!'*)

NEWSREADER. (*Breezily.*) And a very good morning to you! Nothing very startling on the news front today. Still no information on the whereabouts of Frederick Walter, the 'Invisible Man'—whose face nobody has ever seen, the man with seventeen hold-ups to his name, who made a getaway yesterday after seriously wounding two police officers. Road blocks have been set up on all roads in the vicinity. Now the latest on the monetary crisis. The Minister of Finance, after an all night session with the heads of departments of the—

HEAD PORTER. (*Switching off the radio.*) So sorry, sir. My colleague will leave his radio on all night. (*Taking the completed form.*) Thank you, sir. I'll see to your breakfast right away, sir. (*He glances at the form and says importantly.*) Porridge and eggs and bacon, sir?

MAN. (*Surprised.*) No, why? Just coffee and rolls . . .

HEAD PORTER. (*Confused.*) Excuse me, sir. Your name has a British ring to it so I thought . . . We have an international clientele. (*He looks again at the form.*) How silly of me . . . Nationality French! Coffee and rolls, sir, yes. (*He disappears through the service door. The* MAN *continues to look around him, as if surprised to see the place in the light of morning. He sees a shrimping net in the umbrella stand. He takes it, looks at it intently, then crouches down as if he were shrimping on the carpet. Suddenly he sees the* LITTLE BOY *who has come in silently and is standing close by him.*)

MAN. (*With a smile.*) Is this your shrimping net?

BOY. Yes, sir.

MAN. (*Giving it back, kindly.*) I'm sorry. As it's yours and not mine, you must have it back, mustn't you? (*He adds, getting to his feet.*) Besides, you can't catch much on a carpet. I used to like shrimping too, as a boy. You had to get up early, though! Are you going this morning? You wouldn't take me along, would you?

BOY. (*Still gravely, he never smiles.*) If you like.

MAN. (*The* MAN *holds out his hand. The* BOY *takes it, and looks at him gravely. They start to go out, hand in hand into the early morning light.*) Are you here with your mother and father?

BOY. Not my father. He's in Paris. He's working.

My mother's the pianist here . . . (*The* MAN *looks at him without speaking. Just as they are about to go there appears a sort of ageless female tramp, in an old flannel dressing gown, but wearing an amazingly elaborate hat and laden with carrier bags. The* MAN *and* BOY *watch her as she moves timidly towards the service door. The* HEAD PORTER *comes out and goes over to her, furious.*)

HEAD PORTER. You've turned up, haven't you? I told you never to come through the entrance hall! Go round to the back. The kitchen staff will give you your scraps!

OLD WOMAN. (*With a mixture of cunning and timidity.*) It isn't open yet, guv'nor.

HEAD PORTER. (*Seizing her.*) Come back later. Be off, go on! Before the guests see you!

OLD WOMAN. (*With a simpering whine.*) My little pussies are hungry!

HEAD PORTER. You crazy old thing, how many have you got now?

OLD WOMAN. Thirty two, guv'nor. They keep having kittens, you see. (*She gives a toothless smile with a kind of frightening grace to it.*) It's love, guv'nor! Don't you believe in love?

HEAD PORTER. Keep away, you stink!

OLD WOMAN. (*Opening her big, painted eyes with a sort of childlike grace.*) Me, guv'nor? What a nasty thing to say! I've sprayed myself with scent all over . . . It's Cuban Nights—one of the chambermaids had an old bottle she was going to throw in the dustbin . . .

HEAD PORTER. Under the scent is what stinks! My God, how can anybody let themselves go like that? Where's your dignity?

OLD WOMAN. (*With sudden dignity.*) If you'd

known trouble as I have! Anyway, in the afternoon, with my make up on and all my jewellery, I'm not afraid of anybody! I was a beauty once! I was an international beauty queen down on the Coast. The loveliest thighs in Nice! —that's what they said . . . I was a pioneer stripteaser! Rita Zoum! Did you never hear about me?

HEAD PORTER. (*Pushing her out, embarrassed in front of the* MAN.) Oh, that'll do! You and your romancing! Long before my time that was!

OLD WOMAN. (*Simpering toothlessly at the* MAN.) What a way to treat a lady!

HEAD PORTER. Why the management let you in to the roulette tables I'll never know!

OLD WOMAN. (*With dignity, to the* MAN *who looks at her frozen.*) We're all a bit sloppy in the mornings, aren't we, Monsieur? But when I come back to the gaming room in the afternoon, I am spotless! A hotel guest just like anybody else! And my few little winnings are what I live on. We've all got a right to live, haven't we? Just because I've got thirty two cats and I come to the kitchen door for scraps . . . That's my private life! This afternoon, in my frills and lace—why, you won't know me!

HEAD PORTER. (*Sniggering.*) He will by the smell! Go on, hop it. The kitchen's open now. I'll tell you one thing, if it was up to me, you wouldn't set foot in this hotel, with or without your frillies on! The management's too soft with you!

OLD WOMAN. (*Flashing a toothless smile.*) I was very soft with him in days gone by! That's maybe the reason!

HEAD PORTER. (*Nettled.*) I don't want to know. That's not my pigeon. I know my job and I'm doing it. Out, quick.The guests have had their eyeful of you!

(*He seizes her roughly by the wrist. She breaks loose and snaps, with a kind of grandeur.*)

OLD WOMAN. You lackey! Look at it! Does a nose dive when somebody gives it a coin! Want your little tip, do you?

HEAD PORTER. (*Beside himself, but restrained by the presence of the* MAN.) Push off this minute, do you hear? Or I'll report you to the management.

OLD WOMAN. And I shall report you for being rude to a hotel guest!

HEAD PORTER. You a guest?

OLD WOMAN. At three o'clock, with my lace gown on and all my diamonds, I shall be at the tables. Formal dress it says. I shall abide by the rules. Just because I come in the morning, for my cats . . . (*She says with dignity to the* MAN *as she goes.*) Excuse me, monsieur, but this establishment isn't what it was. (*She goes out into the grounds, dragging her leg, and carrying her shapeless bundles.*)

HEAD PORTER. (*Outraged.*) Did you ever see the like! My word, if I was in charge here! Thirty years that creature's been coming here . . . She had a certain splendour it seems, in her time, so they put up with her . . . She lives in a rabbit hutch on the edge of town, with her thirty cats . . . I don't know how she manages out of season, when the place is closed. As soon as we open again, there she is, at the gaming tables, almost clean. She lives off a small legacy from one of the croupiers who used to be here—he must have been her lover at the time . . . Eight hours a day she spends here, placing her tiny little bets . . . She's been here as long as anyone can remember and it seems she left fortunes on the tables, in the old days. . . .

MAN. (*Musingly.*) She must have been very beautiful once . . .

HEAD PORTER. So she says!

MAN. (*To the* SMALL BOY.) Are you coming? Where do you go shrimping now? Is it still the little gully by the breakwater?

BOY. (*Surprised.*) Yes. Why, have you been shrimping here?

MAN. Years ago. (*They go out, hand in hand, through the grounds. A* MAN *of late middle age, very well shaven, looking like a minor official of some sort, comes downstairs into the lobby. The* HEAD PORTER *rushes forward.*)

HEAD PORTER. Good morning, Chief Superintendent! How are we, today, sir? Well, I trust?

SUPERINTENDENT. As well as can be hoped when one's retired . . . You expect to have a rest and you exhaust yourself doing nothing. Ah, old age, what a farce . . . You sleep all day, and lie awake all night.

HEAD PORTER. Now, sir, you're fishing! I never saw a man look so spry. Hale as a youngster, you are.

SUPERINTENDENT. I titivate myself, I have to. But you should see me when I wake up! Ropey as an old boot! Did you listen to the news this morning?

HEAD PORTER. No, I had a client to see to.

SUPERINTENDENT. The Invisible Man's still on the run . . . Invisible man—they make me laugh! It was I who arrested Walter the first time, over twenty years ago . . . After that, when he broke out and went on the run, I was already retired from the Force. And he's buggered up my colleagues ever since.

HEAD PORTER. (*To please him.*) Funny customer, that . . .

SUPERINTENDENT. Handsome fellow. Good face—and that's rare in any circles. He led me a dance, but

I loved it. He wasn't the sort to let you winkle anything out of him, not he! And I've always kept my hands clean. None of your grilling—not even the bright light. Tricks they learnt from the films, all that stuff . . . Just questions, that's all. Only you have to know how to ask them. A pretty game of ping pong we had! You may not believe this but I couldn't wait to get down to the interrogations in the morning . . . We came to have such regard for each other, we'd salute when the other scored a point. I felt quite sad at the end, when I'd nailed him, and he went off with the bracelets on, with those two cretins in uniform barely reaching to his waist! Say what you like, there *is* a hierarchy among men. Social criteria have nothing to do with it.

HEAD PORTER. I was only a lad but I remembered it well. It caused quite a stir at the time!

SUPERINTENDENT. Top police officer in the country, the Minister said, when he commended me. And then, retirement, and that was that. Incidentally, that's the reason I came to be here—as a client, that is. 'The cure? —why not,' said my Doctor. 'If you believe in cures then try it. It's all psychological.' (*He laughs, musing a little.*) He's right, everything *is* psychological, even honesty. I'd come here before to make enquiries about him, years ago. He'd spent a lot of time here as a child and he'd been back with his young wife, some while before his big job . . . There are places that have a pull for you, in some way . . . I always thought he'd come back again. I set my mousetrap and I got him, here in the hotel lobby. I was expecting the usual sort of thug. Not a bit of it! A gentleman! I've always wondered what could have driven him to cross the barrier . . .

HEAD PORTER. (*Puzzled.*) The barrier, sir?

SUPERINTENDENT. Yes. The barrier that separates those we call honest folk from the rest . . . and a very flimsy barrier it is too, when you've been in this job for forty years! I think, you see, that honest folk are the ones who don't dare not to be, mostly. Which one of us hasn't killed someone at least once in his mind? —if only his wife or his mother in law? Only, there are some who really do it. He did. He did the deed and yet he was as innocent as the next man. And my job was to nail him. An ugly weapon, intelligence. Have you ever noticed that?

HEAD PORTER. (*Ingenuously.*) No. I've never had occasion to. (*The* SUPERINTENDENT *rises. He casts a glance into the dining room.*)

SUPERINTENDENT. They're coming down to breakfast. They bore the whiskers off me, these so-called nice people. You couldn't serve me my coffee out on the terrace, could you?

HEAD PORTER. (*With alacrity.*) Certainly, Chief Superintendent, sir! Certainly!

(*The* SUPERINTENDENT *goes out. The* HEAD PORTER *exits through the service door. A family group comes in, laden with scarves, walking sticks, and cameras. The* GRANDMOTHER. *A* YOUNG WOMAN, *with a sad and weary air. One doesn't notice it immediately but she is the same* YOUNG WOMAN *we saw earlier in her night clothes. Her hair is drawn back now, which is enough to give her the necessary age. Two sullen adolescents follow after, a* BOY *and a* GIRL.)

GRANDMOTHER. (*Peeping into the dining room.*) Naturally! They say seven fifteen and they haven't even started serving yet! We'll miss our eight o'clock bus to Le Puys but do they care—not they!

YOUNG WOMAN. I'm sure they'll serve us straight away, mother.

GRANDMOTHER. No they won't. They'll dawdle as usual and we'll miss our bus! And the tea will be lukewarm, you wait and see! This establishment isn't what it was . . . Oh, no, really! —the dining room's locked. Are they afraid we'll steal the cutlery!

YOUNG WOMAN. Don't get excited, mother.

GRANDMOTHER. The waiter at our table has a bandage on his thumb, have you noticed? He dipped it into the soup last night!

YOUNG WOMAN. He cut himself in the kitchen. He told the children.

GRANDMOTHER. Let's hope it isn't a witlow! Did you read about that family in the local papers? —they all got food poisoning from cakes because an assistant pastry-cook had a witlow on his finger? We'll be lucky if we don't end up in hospital!

YOUNG WOMAN. (*Patiently.*) I hardly think it will come to that, mother.

GRANDMOTHER. Call me a pessimist if you like, but I know life. And we've had troubles enough, God knows! I can't imagine what you wanted to come back to this hotel for! It's a mediocre place—always was!

YOUNG WOMAN. I wanted to come back because I was happy here, for one summer. (*She adds.*) Besides, Doctor Bonfant said it would be good for my liver.

GRANDMOTHER. (*With a bitter little laugh.*) Dr. Bonfant is an amiable idiot! My doctor says the cure is absolutely no use at all. This is a third rate hotel with third rate staff, and if you should get some benefit to your liver—which I doubt—you'll lose it all by lapsing back into your chronic depression. This whole area is impossibly dreary and we'd have done better to go to Vichy for my grumbling appendix. Besides, when your husband's left you, as yours did, my poor child—and much shame it's brought on us all—you don't visit the scene of the crime!

YOUNG WOMAN. (*Tersely.*) What happened to me wasn't a crime, it was one of the few happy summers I've ever had.

GRANDMOTHER. (*Bitterly.*) Well, you could have spared your mother that ordeal. When the manager recognised us, after all these years, and he said 'How is Monsieur?' I didn't know where to look. I managed to say 'He's away on business' but I bet he knew.

YOUNG WOMAN. (*Wearily.*) I'm sure he believed you and anyway why should he care?

GRANDMOTHER. You're a saint! You make excuses for everybody. I saw the look in his eye. It isn't only wives who get left. Nobody ever thinks about the mothers-in-law! If you've got a son in law you like to be able to produce him! When I think I was fool enough to take a fancy to that young swine because he looked like an unhappy little boy! (*She sees that the children are listening.*) Jean Christophe, see if the dining room is open yet! (*The* BOY *gets up with a bad grace and crosses the lobby dragging his feet. The* GRANDMOTHER *calls after him.*) And willingly, please, when you're asked to do something!

BOY. (*From the door.*) It's open.

GRANDMOTHER. (*Rising.*) Thank goodness for that! Let's go in. The tea will be cold and the service sloppy as usual, so we'll just be in time to miss our bus. And goodbye to the Cathedral!

YOUNG WOMAN. It's only seven thirty, mother.

GRANDMOTHER. By your watch which doesn't work. Mine does and it says seven thirty five. (*Snapping at the* BOY *as she passes.*) And stand aside for your grandmother! Poor boy, it's not your fault if you never had a father. Nobody taught you to be a gentleman.

YOUNG WOMAN. (*Wearily.*) Don't keep telling them all the time, Mother.

GRANDMOTHER. (*To the* CHILDREN.) You've forgotten your cameras, naturally!

GIRL. (*Sullenly.*) No we haven't.

GRANDMOTHER. Well, that's a surprise! A red letter day this will be, if nothing else happens to spoil it. And lucky we'll be if it doesn't, in my experience! I haven't heard from my lawyer yet, did I tell you? At this rate the thing won't be settled for a year. A wife and five children and some little trollop gives him the eye and everything goes to pot. After fifty all men are pigs! (*They go out into the dining room. The stage is empty for a moment, then the* MOTHER *appears, in her dressing gown, searching. She addresses the* HEAD PORTER.)

MOTHER. You haven't seen my son, have you? I left him asleep in our room. All I did was go to the bathroom and when I came back he was gone!

HEAD PORTER. (*Disobligingly.*) It's not my job to keep an eye on your son! He came down very early and he went off fishing with one of the guests.

MOTHER. Who?

HEAD PORTER. Nobody you know. He arrived last night.

MOTHER. (*Anxiously.*) What sort of man was he? I don't like him going off alone with strangers. There are so many peculiar people about these days.

HEAD PORTER. Oh, you're going it a bit, aren't you?

MOTHER. Don't act so innocent! You meet some pretty queer customers in your job. Look at that English writer last month—the one who kept going up and down in the lift—always forgetting something in his room he said— Well, one evening I was coming down the stairs and I saw him in the lift cage with the young page boy sailing up to seventh heaven. Disgusting old pig! Why don't they stay in England where they belong?

HEAD PORTER. (*Importantly.*) You have to turn a blind eye in my position. The customer is always right.

MOTHER. Yes, but what about your pageboy's fly buttons; are you responsible for them or aren't you?

HEAD PORTER. (*Furious.*) Don't you teach me my job! Twenty years I've been in this trade! And another thing! People in glass houses . . . ! Pardon me for saying so, but if you didn't prowl around the landings in your shift, you wouldn't find your brat missing when you got back to your own room, after getting yourself laid every night!

MOTHER. (*Fuming.*) Listen to him, will you? Don't you lecture me, you oaf! My private life is my business!

HEAD PORTER. (*Nose to nose with her.*) And my business is keeping up the tone of this establishment! For a start you're not allowed to use the passengers' lift! You use the service lift or the back stairs like the rest of the staff!

MOTHER. (*Hands on her hips.*) With the porters, oh great! You don't put floorcloths and serviettes in the same washtub, my fat lad! I fully intend to use the hotel lift and I have made my demands to the management personally!

HEAD PORTER. (*Sniggering.*) I bet! How did you make them—on the green divan in the front office?

MOTHER. You foulmouthed lout! You're scum, you lot—and we're artists!

HEAD PORTER. Artists, my arse!

MOTHER. (*Grabbing him by the collar.*) Do you want a biff on the snout, do you?

HEAD PORTER. Try it—go on! You ignorant slut!

MOTHER. Huh, you watch me!

BOY. (*The* CHILD *has come in, hand in hand with the* MAN. *He has watched the end of the scene. He cries desperately.*) Mother!

MOTHER. (*Dashing over to him and shaking him.*) So, there you are! I've been looking for you everywhere! Go upstairs this minute! I'll teach you to give me a fright like that! You know I've forbidden you to run off without telling me! Go on, quick! Upstairs! (*She slaps his face.*) There!

MAN. (*Intervening.*) We set off to go fishing but we forgot the bait. So we've come back for some . . .

MOTHER. (*Agreeably surprised by the* MAN's *good breeding.*) Oh, I'm not blaming you in the least, Monsieur. But the lad's always running off without telling me . . . Excuse my morning attire . . . I was a little sharp just now, but you know what mothers are, monsieur!

MAN. (*Gravely.*) I do.

MOTHER. (*Simpering.*) Until we meet again, then . . . Very soon I trust. When I shall be rather more respectably dressed, I hope . . . (*She gives the* CHILD *a push.*) Come on! I'll talk to you upstairs!

HEAD PORTER. (*Disgustedly, as he watches her go out.*) All sugar and spice she is now! Quite the lady! And you heard her just now—a proper fishwife! Oh these musicians—what a crew. The management should have had more sense than to let them mix with the guests! But the management's so weak! Madam waggles her hips a bit and she gets anything she wants! It's not my place to say so, sir, but this establishment isn't run the way it used to be! I'd like to have seen the band mingling with the guests when the previous incumbent was in charge!

MAN. (*With a smile.*) Customs change . . .

HEAD PORTER. May be so. But if you love your job, sir, it's hard. I'll order your breakfast, sir, I didn't have a chance to serve it to you before, sir, owing to your leaving the premises, sir. (*He disappears through the service door. The* CHIEF SUPERINTENDENT *has appeared in the doorway, smoking his pipe. He looks steadily at the* MAN *and smiles.*)

SUPERINTENDENT. Lovely day.

MAN. Yes.

SUPERINTENDENT. I was finishing my coffee on the terrace, it's much nicer outside in the sun.

MAN. (*Still smiling.*) Yes. Tomorrow I'll have mine outside too.

SUPERINTENDENT. The little corner, overlooking the thermal baths. That's where you first get the sun in the mornings. Know it?

MAN. Yes.

SUPERINTENDENT. (*With a smile.*) You form your little habits, when you've known a place well, over the years.

MAN. (*Still calm.*) Yes.

SUPERINTENDENT. It's time for my treatment . . . And we're in no hurry, are we? But I'm very much looking forward to our little talk tomorrow morning. It will bring back the good old days.

MAN. Yes.

SUPERINTENDENT. We always exaggerate the importance of the present. We tear this way and that, and in the end we live on memories, as if events, like certain meat dishes, were only really good when heated up. The moment slips through our fingers, shapeless and it's only afterwards, when everything falls into place, that we really savour it . . . And seldom in chronological order—one of man's riper bits of idiocy, that notion, don't you think? Until tomorrow. Or later on today perhaps . . . One goes round in circles here, from the casino to the gardens and back and one invariably meets . . .

(*The* YOUNG MAN *has come downstairs, alone. He stops on seeing the* SUPERINTENDENT. *He is standing close beside the* MAN. *The* SUPERINTENDENT *gives them both a keen look then turns on his heel and goes out unhurriedly into the grounds. The* MAN *and the* YOUNG MAN *stand facing each other. They exchange a long look, as if astonished. The* YOUNG MAN *is the first to break the spell. He goes to the coat stand, takes his raincoat which he left there the night before and goes swiftly out. The* HEAD PORTER, *who has come back to his desk, murmurs as if to himself.*)

HEAD PORTER. He took his raincoat and yet it wasn't raining that day. (*The* MAN *stands there, looking straight ahead. The lighting becomes weird, out of time. The* PORTER *freezes into immobility. The phantom orchestra is heard outside on the bandstand playing an outmoded air which we have already heard in snatches and which we will hear often. The* MAN *listens awhile and murmurs.*)

MAN. That absurd two step . . .

HEAD PORTER. The Washington Post . . . They never played anything else at the time . . . (*A few more bars, then the music fades and the real lighting gradually returns. Reality is further restored by the* HEAD PORTER'S *voice, well and truly alive, talking on the telephone.*) Ten twenty two, Madam. Very well madam, I'll send a page up right away. (*The* FAMILY *comes in wearily, dispirited and laden with paper bags. They flop into armchairs not far from the* MAN.)

GRANDMOTHER. I told you we'd miss the bus! But nobody ever listens to me!

YOUNG WOMAN. Oh mother, we do! Anyway we'd have caught it if the silly child hadn't left her camera on the breakfast table.

GRANDMOTHER. Didn't I say she would? These children! If they can do something stupid they will. Now we'll have to wait for the eleven thirty! Wouldn't you think that driver could have waited? I ran all the way from the square waving my umbrella, don't tell me he didn't see me! And I've twisted my ankle too. Look, it's all swollen! Lovely trip it's going to be! And what a song and dance getting a packed lunch! Too short notice, I ask you! (*She rummages in her paper bag.*) Two hard boiled eggs and a bit of ham! Oh, they've put an apple in—very lavish. Paper napkins naturally! With the price they charge!

YOUNG WOMAN. We did say we'd be having lunch over at Puy. You know you have to tell them the night before if you want a picnic lunch . . .

GRANDMOTHER. The eleven thirty bus will get us there at three and the bus back leaves at five. Three hundred kilometres in this heat and no time to see anything—all because of that little silly!

YOUNG WOMAN. We could always go tomorrow, mother.

GRANDMOTHER. Tomorrow it'll rain.

YOUNG WOMAN. What makes you think that?

GRANDMOTHER. My leg. (*She adds with a mirthless laugh.*) And what about our packed lunches? We'll eat them on a bench out in the grounds, I suppose? We aren't entitled to lunch in the hotel now! (*The*

MAN *looks out from behind his newspaper, which he has tactfully been immersed in since their arrival. He approaches them.*)

MAN. Forgive my intruding—I couldn't help hearing your conversation. As it happens I'm making the same trip myself and I've ordered a car—which is far too big for me—would you allow me to share it with you?

GRANDMOTHER. (*Simpering.*) Oh . . . How too kind of you! My daughter and I are quite overcome . . . But I don't really think . . . We aren't acquainted . . .

MAN. (*Smiling.*) Yes, I only arrived last night, I know . . . But if I'd been here for a week we'd be old friends by now, wouldn't we?

GRANDMOTHER. (*Archly.*) Interesting people are few and far between in these little health resorts, especially at this time of year! I don't see why we shouldn't—do you, Anne Marie? —as this gentleman has so kindly offered . . . but on a fifty-fifty basis—I insist!

MAN. Absolutely not, you must be my guests. I've hired the car anyway.

GRANDMOTHER. (*Capitulating at once.*) Too kind of you, really too kind! My daughter and I are quite overcome, really . . .

MAN. The car will be here at any minute . . . (*To the* YOUNG WOMAN.) You have delightful children, how old are they?

GRANDMOTHER. Fourteen and sixteen. (*To the* CHILDREN.) Stand up when you're spoken to! (*The* CHILDREN *stand up reluctantly and shake hands. The* MAN *looks at them silently for a moment and repeats.*)

MAN. Fourteen and sixteen.

GRANDMOTHER. (*All honey.*) You're a Papa yourself?

MAN. (*Guardedly.*) Yes. I live apart from them though.

GRANDMOTHER. (*Not quite knowing how to take this and deciding to take it sadly.*) Alas! Life is cruel sometimes . . . Why we ourselves—

YOUNG WOMAN. Mother!

HEAD PORTER. The car is here, sir.

MAN. (*Rising.*) Shall we go—if you're ready . . .

GRANDMOTHER. We can't thank you enough, sir! Such a gloomy day it started out to be and now thanks to you, it's turned out quite delightful!

MAN. (*Bringing up rear.*) Don't thank me, it's a great pleasure. It's quite a load sometimes, being alone . . .

GRANDMOTHER. (*Cooing as she goes out.*) Ah, loneliness, loneliness . . . I'm always telling my daughter, she just doesn't realise . . . (*They have gone out. The* SUPERINTENDENT *comes rushing in, calling the* HEAD PORTER.)

SUPERINTENDENT. Leon!

HEAD PORTER. Chief Superintendent, sir?

SUPERINTENDENT. Get me a taxi, will you? I need to take a little trip to Puy.

HEAD PORTER. Ah, the cathedral, sir, yes! One never gets tired of seeing that.

SUPERINTENDENT. (*Watching the others disappear through the grounds.*) Quite so.

HEAD PORTER. Taxi, sir, yes, right away! (*He turns to the telephone.*) Hullo? Casino Hotel here. Send me a car for Puy, will you? The cathedral . . . Yes, another one. They're all going there today! . . .

(*The lights go down. In the halflight the scene changes. Shadowy figures pull away the furniture; set pieces fly up, others fly down: the stylised pillars of the lobby merge with other pillars and grad-*

ually the CATHEDRAL appears. Chairs, prayer stools, a holy water font upstage, in the corner, a tomb, with stone recumbent figure. We are in one of the aisles, with a side chapel. Candles are burning before a statue of the Virgin, which gleams in the half light. A harmonium, distantly heard during the scene change, asserts itself now. The light creeps up. A couple emerges from the gloom, walking slowly. It is the MAN *and the* YOUNG WOMAN. *They appear to be making a tour of the cathedral. They talk without looking at each other.*)

YOUNG WOMAN. And then he ran off with this girl. She was very beautiful and she led him astray . . . They got themselves caught in the end and unfortunately, when the police tried to stop their getaway car, they shot their way out of it . . . And I found myself alone, for good. (*She says, strangely, after a pause.*) Why am I telling you all this? I don't know you. But mother is so garrulous! She started to tell you so many silly stories, I'd rather you knew the truth. I'm not afraid of that.

MAN. (*Murmuring.*) How could he do it?

YOUNG WOMAN. (*A little primly.*) He was very young! That reckless girl . . . she was like strong drink to him. She awoke something in him that he hadn't known was there . . . (*She adds, more genuinely.*) He felt a bit stifled with us, you know. He loved us—the little girl and me—my son wasn't born when he left us . . . . He never knew his father. Oh yes, he loved us, I'm sure he did . . but he felt stifled, that's all. Besides, she was very beautiful . . . Funny, the power beauty has . . . I saw her at the trial. Very beautiful she was, truly, with that lawless urchin look she had . . .

MAN. (*Gently.*) You're beautiful too . . .

YOUNG WOMAN. I was very young when he married me. You know those marriages between childhood sweethearts—you tend to mistake closeness and affection for love . . . And I was a bit prim . . . you know—all knees and elbows and tight as a drum. There were still a few girls like that in those days, in the provinces . . . She was only a year or two older than I, but she'd dipped much deeper into life. (*She says, strangely.*) I wonder what became of her? (*The* MAN *stares straight ahead, without saying anything. She goes on.*) In the grey years that followed—back in childhood with mother, who isn't always easy! —I thought of her often. As often almost—it's funny—as I did of him. I kept the newspaper pictures hidden and every so often, when I was alone, I used to take them out and spend long afternoons, like an idiot, studying the ravishing face of my misfortune . . . (*She adds, comically, in her dry voice.*) You form these unexpected links sometimes, with people!

MAN. (*Heavily.*) She was a sordid little whore, basically commonplace under her arrogance and conceit. They made a film out of their life, I believe. It turned into a very touching love story. Films make heroes out of people like that . . . But when you know them . . . !

YOUNG WOMAN. (*Surprised.*) Did you know her?

MAN. (*Vaguely.*) Later on. I met her after she came out of prison. She was keeping a bar down on the coast. She'd become the mistress of a Marseilles gangster, who was shot at the Liberation, for being a bit too helpful to the Germans. I lost sight of her after that. She'd become a different woman.

YOUNG WOMAN. (*Unexpectedly.*) Had she coarsened a lot?

MAN. (*Smiling at this feminine reaction.*) Would you be pleased if she had?

YOUNG WOMAN. (*With a dry little laugh.*) Yes. Even if you've made a career of sainthood, you're seldom proof against unworthy thoughts!

MAN. She was unrecognisable. Drugs and then—when she couldn't afford that—drink. A hag.

YOUNG WOMAN. (*Lightly.*) How sad.

MAN. (*With a smile.*) Do you mean that?

YOUNG WOMAN. (*Lightly and dryly.*) Like when a lovely thing gets spoiled, let's say . . . But I keep talking about myself, I'm sorry. It's coming to this church . . . it's brought it all to the surface. There are places like that, that haunt you and that one shouldn't go back to . . . (*She adds.*) That one shouldn't go back to again, ever . . . (*She adds in sudden confusion.*) I think we'd better get back to mother and the children . . .

MAN. Here they come. They were with the Superintendent . . .

YOUNG WOMAN. I've let out a lot of confidences. I wonder why . . . I'm usually so close. You've told me nothing about yourself . . .

MAN. (*Evasively.*) A passing traveller . . . And mine's a botched life too, I daresay. Children lost to me for want of a little concern. But what life is a success? It's an appalling phenomenon hindsight, don't you think? (*The* GRANDMOTHER *and the* SUPERINTENDENT *appear, with the bored* CHILDREN *dragging along behind.*)

GRANDMOTHER. They've entirely modernised the church! They've removed practically all of my saints! There are microphones in every corner—as if the Lord's voice wasn't strong enough without! You drop a coin into a slot if you want to light a candle to the

Virgin, just like a fruit machine! And there are piles of catalogues at the door promoting the thing. And that great big kitchen table at the front, with all their paraphernalia, so you can see what they're up to! What times we live in! They've ruined everything for me, even my own God!

SUPERINTENDENT. The world keeps turning, Madame.

GRANDMOTHER. It always has, but in the old days it kept on course. We should never have come back here, Anne Marie . . . The one thing I'll grant is their heating. When I was young divine worship went hand in hand with frozen feet. I must say winter prayers in the warmth does mean progress of a sort.

SUPERINTENDENT. (*Amused.*) You see, there is some.

GRANDMOTHER. Well yes, but it's summer now! (*She continues to wander around.*) I'm curious to see the crypt again. I expect they've put fairy lights round the twelfth century mummies, to make it look more jolly. Are the children coming?

YOUNG WOMAN. Yes, mother.

GRANDMOTHER. Still got their cameras, have they?

YOUNG WOMAN. Yes, mother.

GRANDMOTHER. Well, something else will go wrong, then! It wouldn't be an outing if it didn't. I shall probably sprain my ankle for good and all going down the steps to the crypt.

YOUNG WOMAN. (*A little wearily.*) No you won't, mother. Why do you always want everything to go wrong?

GRANDMOTHER. Because it always does. When you're my age you'll have no doubts about that . . . (*Their voices fade away. They go off, followed by the* CHILDREN. *The* MAN *remains motionless, contemplat-*

ing a row of prayer stools. The SUPERINTENDENT *approaches him and asks.*)

SUPERINTENDENT. Does this place remind you of something?

MAN. (*With a sad little smile.*) Yes. My first love. I was ten. I was in love with a little girl of my own age. I found myself alone with her, here, for the first time. We put our arms around each other, not knowing what we were doing quite. We held each other very close. Her hair had a faint scent of vanilla . . . We didn't dare move, or do anything else. And then her mother caught up with us.

SUPERINTENDENT. Time stands still sometimes . . . (*He adds amused.*) We'll lose the ladies if we dawdle here. They must be in the crypt by now. Are you coming? (*The* MAN *does not move. He goes to him, takes his arm and says more confidentially.*) That's what we are, the sum total of a few moments . . . The myth of the drowning man reviewing his whole life is a farce, of course. One really can't remember it all. We've made so many useless gestures, said so many futile words . . . When you try to think about it, it makes you downright giddy . . . All that expense of energy for nothing—and that's a person's life! But I do think, at the end, that one does relive one or two moments . . . (*He goes on with jaunty good humour, quite unmysteriously.*) I have a theory about that . . . When your heart stops beating and you're dead, medically speaking, there's still one last spurt of blood to the brain, you'll grant me that? That's the mechanics of the thing. So one has one second more of images. One last little look around the memories and then they go. Nevertheless, for a second, with the heart stopped, one's at the centre of that instant. And why should one ever come out of it, since no other instant will ever replace it? Our notion of duration—and very elementary it is, no doubt—only continues to operate for other people now. We go stiff, we start to decompose, they bury us . . . But we remain at the centre of our last state of consciousness because there's no more duration for us. For the others it only lasts a second, but for us it doesn't—the clock has stopped. *That's* eternity! (*He goes on quietly, with a smile.*) So one can conjecture that those who die well, who've only recalled moments of tenderness—you with your little girl companion for instance—are in Heaven. Those who die badly and have seen ugly things are in Hell. Their little personal hell, fixed for eternity. It's a bit idiotic as a theory, but it's no worse than any other . . .

MAN. (*Quietly.*) And those whose life has been a mixture of tenderness and horror?

SUPERINTENDENT. (*Amiably conceding the point.*) Yes, that's where my theory falls down a bit. That would be what Christians call Purgatory. But their Purgatory you get out of, whereas with my last state of consciousness you don't. When you're dead, in my scheme of things, you carry on living forever inside your last little moment. You get no remission for any one of your deeds. And that's not funny! I shall have to see if I can't improve on that a bit . . . (*They have walked away a little. They stop before a tomb in a side chapel.*) The mausoleum of the Lepaud family. Lord of the Manor—they gave a lot of money towards the building of this cathedral. So they were kindly invited in when they were dead. I got to know the last one, in the course of duty. Well, in a manner of speaking. I got to know his corpse. He died of strangulation. It was my last case or nearly. If you're interested in this part of the world, you must have followed the affair in the papers?

MAN. (*Shortly.*) Yes. I did.

SUPERINTENDENT. A well made crime. The vicomte was an old lecher—deflowered half the virgins in the neighbourhood—by ancient privilege perhaps—and then, towards the end, had only one way of reviving his fading powers. . . . No question of honouring the ladies any more, as the quaint old saying goes. Still, you know what men are; right to the end one's hell bent on a little bit of satisfaction for oneself . . . And any means will do. His was the old hanging trick. I daresay you know the legend—which may not be a legend at all—that at the moment of strangulation a man has one last erection followed by a spasm. Do hanged men die at the peak of ecstasy? They'll never tell us. But certain degenerates assert it to be an effective method—if a little violent—and risky. Do you like anecdotes? The last of the Condés, under Louis Philippe, died like that. They found him with his silk scarf round his neck, hanging from the chandelier with his toes scraping the floor. He had a mistress, a local girl who figured largely in his will, and she had a lover too—a real one, who could function without hanging himself. . . . The matter was hushed up, of course. They could do that in those days. But with our viscount we were far more inquisitive. That's democracy. He had a young mistress too. . . . But what am I telling you this for, you know all about it too, don't you?

MAN. (*Neutrally.*) Yes, she was very young and very beautiful.

SUPERINTENDENT. Very. She was the daughter of a local garage owner who supplied the viscount with his Bugattis. The old fellow used to tear about the countryside running over his tenants' chickens. Nobody minded. He paid handsomely in compensation. He paid handsomely for the girl too—cash down to her father . . . He took her into service at fifteen. All he asked of her at first was to wait at table naked with pink ribbons round her thighs. And then, of course, he proceeded to enlist her help in his ultimate attempts at bliss. Needless to say the girl—outside her hours of work—if you can call it that—had lovers pretty well everywhere.

MAN. (*Neutrally.*) Pretty well, yes.

SUPERINTENDENT. (*Casually.*) And then, one day, she got attached to one of them. A young fellow, as different from her as chalk from cheese, married to a girl from a very respectable county family, father of a little girl. Perhaps it was his very honesty that amazed her. Delinquents mystify us, but we mystify delinquents too, even if they pretend to despise us a bit . . . And a great mutual attraction, of course; nothing happens without that. In short, they thought they'd found love eternal. At least he did.

MAN. (*Oddly.*) Yes. He particularly.

SUPERINTENDENT. Whereupon the viscount had his little accident.

MAN. (*Neutrally.*) Why a crime though? The girl wasn't going to inherit anything. All they had to do was go away together, that's all.

SUPERINTENDENT. That was one of the arguments the defence brought forward at the trial. But, among other bad habits, the girl had developed a taste for money, with her elderly protector. She'd long since stopped waiting at table, with her pink thigh ribbons. She was the titular mistress, despised in the neighbourhood, but feared. Quite a night life she had, in the high spots hereabouts, gambling chiefly, in the local casinos. An aristocratic craving she acquired from her aged Viscount. She went through some pretty massive sums at the tables.

MAN. (*Neutrally.*) They left without taking anything though. The enquiry proved that.

SUPERINTENDENT. Yes, but they had a huge amount to live on, from somewhere. That's why I was asked to resume investigations. And that's when I discovered something extremely interesting, when I had the advantage of meeting the viscount on the occasion of his interment . . . (*He stops suddenly, waving the subject away with a smile.*) But that's an old, long buried story, if I may risk a little joke. You want to watch out for old lads like me; when they start to mull over their memories they never stop . . . Let's go and join the ladies, I'm sure they're wondering where we've got to . . . And then we'll take the children out to tea. Fine children, aren't they? A bit strange, though. And very much turned in on themselves, don't you think?

MAN. Yes.

SUPERINTENDENT. Can you wonder, growing up without a father?

(*They have moved out of sight among the gloom of the pillars. A harmonium is heard. A choir of children's voices, shrill and uncertain, rehearsing a hymn somewhere in the distance. The voices fade away. Later, the choir will take up another chant, far away, creating an air of unreality in the deserted church. The revolving door opens upstage, admitting a ray of light. A graceful figure appears, in a headscarf, dressed in an anorak from which emerge the bare legs of a young country girl. She is very young and very beautiful. The part is played by the actress who played the* TRAMP *at the beginning but this one cannot notice straightaway. She goes to a prayer stool and kneels. Soon the* YOUNG MAN *emerges from the darkness in his raincoat, just as we saw him leave the hotel. He hesitates then goes to kneel by the girl on an adjacent stool. The choir is heard in the distance. They both cast a glance round the empty church before they start to talk in low voices. The* SUPERINTENDENT *and the* MAN *who were about to leave when the* GIRL *came in, stand and watch them in the gloom at the back of the church.*)

YOUNG MAN. Why did you ask me to meet you here?

GIRL. It's cool. The heat's killing outside . . . There's a huge storm brewing! . . . Anyway, it's fun, seeing you in church . . . Besides, it's safer. You don't know him. He has spies everywhere. He's the king of the county. There isn't a garage mechanic, not a cafe owner—he's known them all since they were so high—who wouldn't have gone to him and said 'Hey, your Lordship sir, your young lady from the big house, we saw her yesterday with a young man!' Tomorrow they'll say 'Hey, your Lordship, sir, going to confession now is she, that young lass of yours?' That will surprise him a bit, but it'll make him giggle, the old pervert, when he imagines all the things I could be telling the priest!

YOUNG MAN. What will you say when you get back?

GIRL. I'll say I got too hot when I was shopping and the cathedral was the only cool place there was. It's true, it's the only cool spot in this damn town in summer! (*She casts a furtive glance round.*) It's nice being in a church—not that I ever go! Did you when you were small?

YOUNG MAN. Yes.

GIRL. My father kept a garage, he used to get all

the Viscount's Bugattis for him. The old man was his chief customer and he'd quake at the sight of him. But that didn't stop him voting red and yelling 'Down with the priests!' from morning till night. He wouldn't let me be baptised, nor make my First Communion. Oh I was so miserable—because of the dress, you see! All the girls at school were as lovely as brides. I'm drawn to churches now . . . The old man knows that. That's why I shan't have any bother if he finds out. Otherwise, out comes the riding whip, if he suspects I've cheated on him!

YOUNG MAN. (*Heavily.*) You're young and you're beautiful and he's old. Anyone would think you were his slave!

GIRL. (*Softly.*) It's a bit like that, you know . . . He paid for me, cash down, at fifteen, and he who pays the piper . . . (*She adds, hard.*) But I frighten him too now. (*A pause. She says softly.*) Touch me. Put your hand under my skirt . . . Useful things, prayer stools . . . Do you know, he's got a chair, the dirty old pig, a queer thing it is. Some king in the old days, just as disgusting as him, gave it to one of his ancestors. He'd had it made specially . . . It's worth a fortune, there are only five or six like it in the world . . . it's half like a bidet and half like a prayer stool: it's called a pleasuring chair. The things men can think up—it's really twisted!

MAN. (*Getting to his feet, as if hurt.*) Let's get out of here.

GIRL. (*Holding him back.*) Stay where you are. We'll be seen if we go outside. It's market day. Touch me. (*He doesn't move. She asks insidiously.*) The church is empty. What are you afraid of, little boy? The little red lamp?

YOUNG MAN. No.

GIRL. Are you afraid of love, if it isn't just so, with nice clean pyjamas, in a nice tidy bed? You've taken me on the floor mostly, or up against a wall, haven't you, up till now?

YOUNG MAN. (*Heavily.*) I don't want that man to touch you any more.

GIRL. (*Softly, after a pause.*) That depends on you, I told you that . . . Otherwise tonight, like every other night . . . I told you, didn't I, how the old skinflint gets me to earn my necklace—a pearl at a time? For what he wants, I don't have to go very far, but it's always very complicated . . . (*She adds suddenly sly.*) I love it when you look like that, my puss cat . . . I love to see it hurting you when you think of him! (*The* YOUNG MAN *gets to his feet suddenly, pale faced, and hits her.* GIRL, *surprised, with some respect.*) Do you often hit girls in church? (*She clings to him, tenderly stroking his neck.*) I love you. You're the one I belong to. But you'll have to take me, really take me.

YOUNG MAN. (*Heavily.*) We'll leave tonight.

GIRL. (*Softly and insidiously.*) Have you any money?

YOUNG MAN. I'll find some.

GIRL. (*Softly.*) I need a great deal, you know, I've got into bad ways . . . (*She adds hard-voiced.*) What about your dear little wife and your dear little girl, my cherub?

YOUNG MAN. I'm leaving them.

GIRL. (*In an undertone.*) Kneel down. There's an old woman taking a candle into the Lady chapel. (*They keep very still, hands joined in prayer, while an* OLD WOMAN, *barely distinguishable, passes close by in the dark and goes to light a candle at the adjacent altar. The* GIRL *says under her breath.*) That's the chair attendant. If he's got her in his pocket then we're for it. He never sets foot inside a church but I wouldn't put anything past him, crafty old devil! You know it was his family gave all the money to build this cathedral, centuries back? Their tomb's over there in the corner, do you want to see it? (*She pulls him over to the tomb.*) Isn't it funny, it might be him, lying there—with a beard. (*She adds, slyly.*) Only, when I see him lying on his back like that, he's not in armour. Just lots of flabby little creases on his chest and his revolting old belly, with the veins all sticking out . . . (*She gives a wicked little laugh.*) That's a bit like armour, too, really—an old man's skin . . . You get used to it, of course—you get used to everything!

YOUNG MAN. (*Tensely.*) I'll talk to my wife when I get back. I don't want to go without talking to her. I'll tell her I can't go on any more. I'll be at the end of the big lime walk tonight at eleven with the car. Bring one small suitcase, that's all. I don't want you to take anything of his.

GIRL. (*With a smile.*) I'll come naked then? (*She asks again.*) Have you got some money?

YOUNG MAN. Enough to go away with, yes. After that I'll work, I'll find some sort of job.

GIRL. Very convenient, your mamma in law's factory, wasn't it? You're not trained for anything.

YOUNG MAN. (*With a strangled cry.*) I won't have that man touching you ever again!

GIRL. (*With a smile.*) I can just hear you when you were little, my pet. I don't want to go to school, I don't want to go to the office, I don't want to do my military service! Ah but we have to just the same . . . Haven't you learnt that yet? (*She adds with sudden harshness.*) If you wanted to, if you really loved me, we could do it . . . Only you'll need a bit of courage and you'll have to forget what you read in your schoolbooks . . . (*A growl of thunder is heard and the sound of heavy rain.*) Listen, there's the storm at last. It's coming down like a pissing horse, there won't be a stray cat in the streets now. We'll run out to your car and and you'll take me to our little wood. We'll be quiet there and I'll explain everything. Come on. That old woman's getting on my nerves prowling around like that. It'll be nice out there in your car. (*She puts her arms round him and murmurs.*) And I want you now. And you want me. I can always tell when you look at me that way . . .

YOUNG MAN. (*Murmuring.*) How beautiful you are . . . (*He kisses her, and when they break apart we see a nightmare sight. He is holding in his arms the smiling, enticing old* TRAMP WOMAN *we saw at the beginning of the play.*)

OLD WOMAN. Come on, come quick, puss cat. We'll never get to the wood! And give me some holy water on the way out, little choirboy, go on. I adore that! Wet fingers touching and a hot sideways look, you don't need to do much else sometimes . . . (*She gives a little laugh, with her frightening airs and graces.*) Trust your pious little pink and white virgins to invent a way of making love on the sly, with their fingertips. (*She draws him away.*)

MAN. (*Leaps forward, shouting.*) Stop! (*They stop, in surprise; and look round, seeing no one.*)

YOUNG MAN. It's all right, there's nobody there. Come, beloved. (*He pulls her away, leaving the* MAN *standing there, nonplussed.*)

MAN. (*Murmuring.*) We've got to tell him who it is he's going away with!

SUPERINTENDENT. (*Joining him, with a smile.*) He's going with youth and love . . . And they travel fast!

When I arrested them both she was still very young and lovely and the night I interrogated her, it took all my professional conscience not to fall into her net! An old fox like me, who could nose out guilt a mile off, and there I was snared by her blinding innocence . . . Curious animals, men! They build systems and empires, give their lives with a smile for an idea. Talk with God and then suddenly, off they go, just anywhere, with just anybody—dragged by the slit in their breeches. Lightweights, all of them. (*The* MUSICIANS *come into the church, noisy and ludicrous.*) Ah, here come the buskers. They'd planned to visit the cathedral that day as well. That's humanity for you too. (*The* MUSICIANS *spread out in groups round the cathedral. Behind them, the* LITTLE BOY, *alone and forlorn. The two* OLD MUSICIANS *pass each other holy water, fooling about at the font.*)

1ST MUSICIAN. Are you going fishing?

2ND MUSICIAN. No. I'm going fishing.

1ST MUSICIAN. Sorry. I thought you were going fishing.

GIRL MUSICIAN. (*Indignantly.*) Have you finished mucking about, you two? Christ, don't you have any respect for anything? A church is a church!

1ST MUSICIAN. Not any more it isn't. What with priests getting married and prancing about in shorts, they can belt up with their holy talk. We're all mates now!

GIRL MUSICIAN. (*To her girl friend.*) Listen to him, will you? Filthy old devil.

1ST MUSICIAN. It's a fact. I made my First Communion like everybody else. I long since stopped going to Mass, but there was a little something left. They did it all with their backs to you on the high altar then, in Latin. But now, it's down front on a big table, and you can understand every word. Well, how can you take their God seriously now? I'll tell you, the script wasn't half as good as we thought!

GIRL MUSICIAN. (*Wandering round arm in arm with her friend.*) Just look at that window, isn't it gorgeous.

2ND GIRL. And the Virgin's robe! That mauve!

1ST GIRL. Of course, being fair . . . It wouldn't suit a brunette.

2ND MUSICIAN. It's like music. You get some who set Mozart and Beethoven to jazz . . . and that's put finish to music! They're scuttling their own boat too. It's the fashion these days!

1ST GIRL. Be quiet, you two! Can't you keep your dirty talk for the bar!

2ND GIRL. Those two! We can't even look round a cathedral in peace!

1ST MUSICIAN. And take confession. A fellow who fondles his nancy and frisks about the same as you—would you feel like telling him about your own goings on? What right has he got?

1ST GIRL. In the first place I've got nothing to confess, not to anybody! My lovers are my affair.

1ST MUSICIAN. (*Spluttering with laughter.*) Oh, the wicked thing! Saying that in church! Had lovers, has she? Who would have guessed! (*They move off to look at the church.*) Have you seen the big organ? Early seventeenth century. Only two others of its size in the country. And all that just to pep up the hymn tunes for the faithful to swing to! (*They go out. The* LITTLE BOY *remains alone, in the background.*)

2ND GIRL. Isn't it lovely though? They thought big in those days!

1ST GIRL. Yes, but it's damp. I knew I was right to bring my jacket!

2ND GIRL. What's that little red lamp up there?

1ST GIRL. That's Our Lord.

2ND GIRL. (*Amazed.*) Strewth, is he always there?

1ST GIRL. The thing I love is the candlelight. Electricity's ruined everything, it's a shame . . . (*They move on. They are heard, further off, by the tomb.*)

2ND GIRL. Who's that old fellow lying there? Is he a saint?

1ST GIRL. No, he's a nobleman. Can't you see his sword?

2ND GIRL. What's he doing there, then?

1ST GIRL. I dunno. (*To the* BOY, *as she goes.*) Are you coming?

BOY. Where's my mother?

1ST GIRL. (*Moving off arm in arm with her friend.*) She stayed in the cafe with Alberto. They didn't feel like coming. Alberto wasn't well. He's got a pain. (*They have disappeared. The* SUPERINTENDENT *and the* MAN *look at the* BOY, *who stands there alone, and still.*)

SUPERINTENDENT. (*Murmuring.*) Endearing little lad, don't you think, with that tragic look of his? . . . (*The* BOY *has knelt down. He makes the sign of the cross and says in a low intense voice.*)

BOY. Please God, make him die. Please God, make him die. Please God, make him die. I'll never ask You for anything ever again but make him die! (*He breaks into sobs, bent over his prayer stool. Moved, the* MAN *makes to go up to him. The* SUPERINTENDENT *holds him back.*)

SUPERINTENDENT. No. There's nothing you can do for him. You know that.

MAN. (*Murmuring.*) He's too alone.

SUPERINTENDENT. We're all alone. He's learning. (*An unknown* LITTLE GIRL *in an old-fashioned dress comes on, looking for someone. She stops beside the* LITTLE BOY.)

LITTLE GIRL. Are you crying? I've been looking for

you. I ran away while Mother was buying holy pictures. (*The* BOY *has not moved, his small face closed and set. She gives his head a little stroke.*) I don't want you to cry. When we're grown up we'll get married and I'll make you happy. (*The* BOY *has straightened. They stand facing each other, motionless and shy. Then, suddenly, with very slow movements, full of a kind of grave modesty, their arms go round each other and they stand in close embrace. The* LITTLE GIRL *says softly:*) We won't ever be alone again, when we're married.

BOY. (*He says nothing at first, then he says mysteriously.*) This time, I really have killed him.

LITTLE GIRL. Really and truly?

BOY. Yes. I put something in his glass. If they put me in prison will you still love me?

LITTLE GIRL. (*Softly.*) Yes.

BOY. Even if they cut my head off?

LITTLE GIRL. (*Gravely.*) Yes. I'll always love you.

BOY. It took him in the bus. He's in the cafe now, all stiff. They laid him down on top of a table and he's dead. Mamma's crying.

LITTLE GIRL. Did it hurt him, do you think?

BOY. (*Gravely.*) He suffered horribly.

LITTLE. GIRL. (*Quietly.*) Serves him right.

BOY. Yes.

ALBERTO. (*Suddenly the light shows at the back as the door opens. Heavy footsteps are heard.* ALBERTO *appears.*) So there you are, you little moron. Your mother's been looking everywhere for you. She thought you'd been drowned. She had a thousand fits again. Come on, get moving! We'll miss the bus! (*As he drags him roughly out, the* GRANDMOTHER *appears. She is visibly younger and dressed much more showily, in the fashion of the thirties, and with indisputably bad taste.*)

GRANDMOTHER. Anne Marie, what are you at? I've been looking for you everywhere! What do you mean by giving your mother such a fright? Come on, hurry, we'll miss the bus! (*Dragging her off.*) You know I've forbidden you to hang about with that boy from the orchestra!

LITTLE GIRL. But Mamma, he's very nice.

GRANDMOTHER. That's not the point. He's not our class. (*The two* CHILDREN *have been dragged off on opposite sides. The bus is heard hooting outside in the square. The* MUSICIANS *cross the stage, running.*)

1ST MUSICIAN. Let's get moving kids, we'll miss that bus!

GIRL. (*Crossing with the other one.*) I told you it was worth the trip! You stagnate, always loafing about in cafes between shows. A cathedral now and again does you a power of good! (*At the holy water font the two* MUSICIANS *can't resist repeating their joke as they pass each other holy water.*)

1ST MUSICIAN. You going fishing?

2ND MUSICIAN. No, I'm going fishing.

1ST MUSICIAN. Oh, I thought you were going fishing! (*They go out. The* MAN *and the* SUPERINTENDENT *are alone. The* SUPERINTENDENT *says quietly.*)

SUPERINTENDENT. Suppose you and I went fishing now, Frederick Walter, like the two old acquaintances we are?

MAN. (*Holding out his wrists with a little smile.*) It's taken you a long time . . .

SUPERINTENDENT. (*Not moving, with a little smile too.*) No. There are no handcuffs in my pocket. I'm retired. This is just for the fun of it.

(*The curtain falls on the two men, as they stand looking at each other, motionless and faintly smiling.*)

END OF ACT ONE

ACT TWO

The lobby of the Casino Hotel. It is raining—one hears the rain all through the beginning of the scene—and the HEAD PORTER *can be seen escorting the guests with a big red umbrella.*

The orchestra is up on a rostrum, giving their concert inside the building.

At a table, downstage, the GRANDMOTHER *(Anne Marie's mother, young, as we saw at the end of the last act) is taking tea with the* LITTLE GIRL *and the* LITTLE BOY. *At a nearby table, a little apart, the* MAN *and the* SUPERINTENDENT *are watching them.*

As the curtain rises, the band is finishing a sentimental number. The WAITER *comes to take the order.*

WAITER. And for the young man?

GRANDMOTHER. (*Smoothly.*) You don't want anything, do you, Frederick?

BOY. No, Madame.

GRANDMOTHER. (*Dismissing the* WAITER.) Very sensible of you, this tea is undrinkable. This place wouldn't know a boiling kettle if it saw one . . . Any way, why order another pot? This one's as big as a chamber pot. You could use Anne Marie's cup, she's finished hers. And thank Heaven—they're mean with the butter and jam—but they're not stingy with the sugar, it's full of fly dirt but there's plenty. Two lumps? (*She pours out, with little finger cocked.*)

BOY. Yes please.

GRANDMOTHER. Anne Marie, if you don't want your tart, perhaps Frederick would like it? (*The* LITTLE GIRL *passes her tart to the* BOY *who eats it while they look at each other gravely on either side of the* GRANDMOTHER.) It's good to see a little boy enjoying his food! Do you get full board as well as your mother, in the hotel?

BOY. Yes, Madame.

GRANDMOTHER. (*Cheerfully.*) Judging by the way they stint the guests, I can imagine how they feed the staff! Eat up my boy, eat up! At your age you need to build up your strength. Anyway Anne Marie would have left half of it. She's spoilt to death, I'm afraid. Children from poorer homes are much healthier in the long run. Eat, my boy, take what you can get while you can. What did they give you for lunch?

BOY. Mutton.

GRANDMOTHER. (*With an acid little laugh.*) I can just see it. Our last night's leftovers. Mark you I'm delighted. If they hadn't got the staff to force it down we'd have had it served up again as meatballs. This hotel has gone down dreadfully. (*She studies him with interest and asks, suddenly sympathetic.*) What do you do with yourself, my poor lad, while your mother's busy with the orchestra?

BOY. (*Uncommunicatively.*) I go for walks.

GRANDMOTHER. (*With a meaningful sigh.*) All on your own, poor boy? And in the evenings?

BOY. I go to bed and wait for my mother to come in.

GRANDMOTHER. You share a room, do you?

BOY. Yes, Madame.

GRANDMOTHER. Aren't you afraid, all by yourself on the sixth floor? It must be deserted up there?

BOY. I can hear the band out in the grounds. I try to stay awake until she comes in. Sometimes the music sends me to sleep . . . But I don't like that because then I don't know when she comes in.

GRANDMOTHER. Poor child. And your father?

BOY. He's in Paris. Working.

GRANDMOTHER. What does he do?

BOY. He's a tailor.

GRANDMOTHER. (*Plying an imaginary needle.*) He sews suits, does he?

BOY. (*Hurt.*) No! He doesn't sew! The coat hands and the trouser hands do that! He's a cutter! He's got great big scissors, and coloured chalks and rulers and great big books bound in red leather with all the patterns in! But he doesn't even look at them now! The machinists and the finishers do the sewing, bent over a table. My Father works standing up. He's a master cutter!

GRANDMOTHER. (*Indifferent to these finer points.*) Oh really . . . I didn't know there was any difference . . . Was the tart good?

BOY. Yes thank you.

GRANDMOTHER. There, you see, Anne Marie, when you're hungry enough, you eat. Spoilt little girls are never hungry. Money doesn't make for happiness, you know!

BOY. (*Crying out, stung again.*) I'm spoilt too! Mother gives me too much money!

GRANDMOTHER. (*With a smile.*) Why, my poor child, who told you that?

BOY. (*Back in his shell again.*) My mother's friend. The one who plays the saxophone.

GRANDMOTHER. (*With a knowing smile.*) Poor boy.

(*The band, which had stopped, now starts to play again.*)

SUPERINTENDENT. (*To the* MAN.) Admirable thing the bourgeoisie. It's the only social class that's found the answer to everything. Aristocrats and workers who are more alike than they think, live from week to week. The middle class, which has taken two centuries to nibble away at the first lot and sat its big bum solidly on the others, can now devote itself entirely to its good conscience. That little girl's mother is treating herself under our very eyes to the delights of charity—with a cup of cold tea and a bit of apple tart. Look at her, clucking like a contented hen, with her pearls gleaming on her fat lace front . . . She's doing a bit of social work, over afternoon tea. She's helping a poor underprivileged lad, with great generosity, to hoist himself one notch up out of the gutter. (*The* GRANDMOTHER *goes on with her edifying monologue, only snatches of which are heard, mingled with the music of the band.*)

GRANDMOTHER. For there's one thing that's very important, Frederick, and that's doing as much as one possibly can for one's fellow men. It's more than a pleasure, it's a duty.

MAN. (*Murmuring, with his gaze fixed on the nearby table.*) Did you hear how he shouted "I'm spoilt too?" He loathes her at this moment and he'll carry that with him all his life. He'll never forgive rich middle aged women for anything, ever.

SUPERINTENDENT. (*Gently.*) Yes, but he's in love with the little girl.

MAN. Yes, he's in love with the little girl and he's looking at her. And he's happy just the same, while the mother goes on with her edifying monologue. He doesn't care, he can't hear her now.

GRANDMOTHER. Take me. Now I could very well have thought of nobody but myself. That's all too easy when you have money . . . Well, not a bit of it . . . I've always forced myself to think of those less fortunate than I was. And there's no merit in it. Charity is a pleasure too.

SUPERINTENDENT. He's in love with the little girl and he may marry her one day—who knows? When he's grownup, and thinks that that's what happiness is . . .

GRANDMOTHER. It's a great joy to know you've always done your duty.

SUPERINTENDENT. And then he'll notice that his wife is slowly turning into a milder version of her mother and that he's finding it difficult to breathe . . .

MAN. (*Strangely.*) You know the whole story . . .

SUPERINTENDENT. It only takes a little imagination. (*The band have finished their number. Polite applause.*)

GRANDMOTHER. (*To the* BOY.) Why, that was a very pretty piece. The piano solo was very good. Your Mamma is an excellent artist. Whatever made her think of playing in a band?

BOY. She used to give piano lessons. When my father went away to the war she had to take a full time job.

GRANDMOTHER. War is a dreadful thing. For everybody. Anne Marie's father was a major in the Cavalry. I had to take over the management of the factory myself, in nineteen fourteen. He died for his country in nineteen sixteen, on the Somme. And I went on running the business as a widow. I'm a good Frenchwoman. I've always done my duty.

BOY. (*With a violent cry.*) My mother's always done her duty too!

(*The dance floor has been cleared. A hotel page goes round handing paper hats and streamers to the children present. The band strikes up the "Skaters' Glide." Child couples in paper hats get up from the tables.*)

GRANDMOTHER. Anne Marie, it's Thursday today—time for the children's dance. And it's the Skaters' Glide—just what M. Galempoix taught you last term. Why don't you ask your little friend to dance? Can you dance, Frederick? Have you had lessons?

BOY. No, Madame. I taught myself.

GRANDMOTHER. Why then, let's see how well you do at it. Go along, children, dance, you're the age for it. (*The children all start to dance, fondly watched by their mothers. It is a rather silly but graceful little dance. The* MAN *watches the little couple dancing and murmurs as if in a dream.*)

MAN. You don't touch each other much in the Skaters' Glide—the steps are a little stylised, but perhaps the band will play a polka; then he can hold her close in the soft vanilla scent of her . . . she will get a little hot—the polka is a fast dance—and she will have little halos of sweat under her gauzy dress and they will smell sweet too . . . (*The band has switched imperceptibly to a very lively polka to which the little boy and girl begin to dance as if possessed. The* MAN *goes on.*) He taught himself but he's the better dancer . . . His white socks are spotless; he flew into a temper with his mother because she washed them too late in the washbasin this morning; they're still a little damp but it doesn't show—he knows he's the handsomest boy in the room and everyone is looking at him . . . He's no longer the pianist's son, who's always a little bit ashamed for people to know why he's here, with the others, whose fathers and mothers are guests in the hotel . . . They don't need to invent for themselves—as he does sometimes—imaginary parents who are away on a trip that day . . . He's a young guest himself at the moment . . . And that's what he'll be aiming for all his life, perhaps because of this one afternoon. And he'll do everything on earth, just to achieve it.

SUPERINTENDENT. (*Quietly.*) Yes. Everything, exactly. Which will lead him into making my acquaintance. (*He watches them for a while longer. The little couple start to act in a very strange way. They no longer follow the rhythm of the music, as do the others who are still dancing round them: their movements have slowed down as if in a dream.*)

MAN. She's full of warmth against him and her slight little body smells sweet . . . Perhaps that's what those others in the band are always talking about? . . . Perhaps that's making love? . . . He has laid her on the ground, right there, in the midst of all the others who are dancing . . . He puts his full weight on her and then suddenly—he has only seen animals do it—he doesn't know if he has to go on moving or just lie there, as she pants gently—with all his weight on her . . .

(*The little boy and girl are lying on the dance floor in the midst of the other children who are dancing under the adults fond gaze. The music stops. They get up, red with embarrassment and go back to the table where Anne Marie's mother, who has not taken her eyes off them, greets them complacently behind her lorgnette.*)

GRANDMOTHER. Why, that was perfect, children. You looked very sweet both of you. You dance very well, Frederick, for a boy who's never had lessons. You see, Anne Marie? And you were so slow to pick it up, even with the best dancing master in town. I hope you'll do as well in your schoolwork, Frederick. Are you a scholarship boy?

BOY. Yes, Madame.

GRANDMOTHER. Very good. When one comes from a modest background it's merit that counts. (*She looks at the band through her lorgnette.*) That's the interval . . . The musicians are putting their instruments away and I think your mother's looking for you, Frederick . . . I'll let you go now . . . (*The* MUSICIANS *come down off the rostrum.*)

MUSICIANS. We're entitled to our drinks. If they say they're too busy like last time then they can whistle for their tips at the end of the week. Once, down in Antibes it was, one of them refused to serve me. 'Listen son,' I said, 'How long did you study before you learnt to carry a tray? I worked for five years at the double bass.' That soon shut him up.

GIRL. This time I'm asking for a cherry brandy. And if he says we're only allowed beer I'm going straight to the management.

MUSICIANS. A drink is a drink. Union rules. It's in the contract. Did you see those children jigging about? In this heat! At that age your feet don't hurt. (*They have gone out through the service door. The* LITTLE BOY *has joined his* MOTHER.)

MOTHER. What were you doing at that table? You know you're not supposed to talk to the guests. You'll get me into trouble again.

BOY. The mother of the little girl I play with in the gardens asked me.

MOTHER. (*Anxiously.*) You behaved yourself I hope? You know you eat like a pig half the time. You didn't go and disgrace me? I must go and thank the lady.

BOY. (*Horrified.*) No, Mother, don't!

MOTHER. Of course I must, it's only polite! (*She goes to the table where* ANNE MARIE'S MOTHER *greets her from her seat with smiling condescension.*) Allow me to introduce myself. I'm Frederick's mother and I wanted to thank you for asking him to your table . . . I do hope he wasn't a nuisance?

GRANDMOTHER. Oh he was perfect. Anyway it's the least I could do. Always on his own, poor child, one feels so sorry for him. He's a charming little boy and very well brought up I must say. Such good manners.

MOTHER. (*Gurgling.*) One does one's best, you know.

GRANDMOTHER. Do you want to make a musician of him, like yourself?

MOTHER. I don't think he cares for music . . . But his father and I hope to get him through college. His father would like him to be an engineer.

GRANDMOTHER. A very good idea, industry is developing at such a rate! I'm sure he'll rise above his present circumstances and be a great credit to you. My little girl is very fond of him and we'd be very happy if you'd let us have him from time to time. The poor little lad is always so lonely.

MOTHER. (*With great distinction, simpering.*) Thank you Madame, very many thanks.

GRANDMOTHER. (*Overcome by her own good nature.*) Oh no, no, no, please! One's only too happy if one can do a good turn now and again. (*They both simper.* ALBERTO, *who has been waiting, comes up to them and cuts short the civilities.*)

ALBERTO. You coming then, my duck? There's just time for a quick one. (*A second of embarrassment, then the* MOTHER *with one last distinguished smile lets herself be borne away.*)

MOTHER. Do please excuse me, won't you?

GRANDMOTHER. (*With a thin smile.*) Madame . . . (*The little* BOY *and* GIRL *have moved towards each other while the mothers were talking. The boy points to the receding pair.*)

BOY. Look. He can't walk properly. I arranged for a double dose this time. The man who washes the glasses in the bar is a friend of mine. That's who he goes to cadge his drinks from. He won't be back with the band after the interval. They'll start to play without him—then they'll get worried and go and look—and they'll find him in the lavatory dead . . .

LITTLE GIRL. (*Gravely.*) Serve him right.

GRANDMOTHER. Come children, let's get some air while the band's out. The heat in here! It shouldn't be beyond the wit of man to open the windows and draw the blinds down! But that would make work for the staff—so the guests' comfort can go hang! (*She goes out, followed by the children. The room has emptied. Only the* MAN *and the* SUPERINTENDENT *who have been following it all from their table, remain onstage.*)

SUPERINTENDENT. I'm reconstructing it all slowly . . .

MAN. (*With a kind of sombre humour.*) Me too! What a time it takes to understand . . .

SUPERINTENDENT. A lifetime. And then, the moment one's grasped it—pfutt! (*He draws closer to him with a touch of malice.*) You and I might be of some help to each other—what do you think? That's the ideal interrogation. Truth is so difficult to catch by the tail for everybody . . . For the culprit as well as for the policeman sometimes . . . Except that they're not working towards the same end. That's why it's heads or tails whether you get acquitted or condemned. (*He gives a little laugh.*) When it comes down to it, they should only prosecute in cases where there's a time limit. The law might have a slight chance of getting somewhere then . . . So you came back that evening, in your car, to wait for her at the end of the lime walk. You were going away with her—was that the plan?

MAN. Yes.

SUPERINTENDENT. And she came down to the car with her suitcase?

MAN. Yes. (*He says with sudden unaccustomed tenderness.*) It was too heavy for her; but there was a moon and I could have been seen from the windows, so I had to let her carry it into the shadow . . . She was exhausted, and frightened. All of a sudden she was a little girl, and her so insolent always . . . She flew into my arms, with her heart thumping, and suddenly something happened, something I'd never imagined could happen with her . . . I'd only ever felt desire for her, but now I was flooded with tenderness, with a need to protect her. I'd never been anything but a selfish little rake chasing his own pleasure. It was that night I think at that minute, that I became a man.

SUPERINTENDENT. At that minute you could still have left. She asked you to go back up with her?

MAN. Yes.

SUPERINTENDENT. Why?

MAN. He wasn't asleep, he was waiting for her in his room . . . She had used the time while he was preparing for bed to take her suitcase down, but she had to go back up or he might send someone out to look for her. She begged me to wait, she wouldn't be long she said . . . But I couldn't stay there hiding in the car while that man might be mauling her. I followed her up.

SUPERINTENDENT. With her consent?

MAN. No, she didn't want me to, she was afraid, but she couldn't stop me.

SUPERINTENDENT. Why did either of you go up at all?

MAN. I don't know. It was absurd.

SUPERINTENDENT. And when you got there?

MAN. She made me wait in a dark little dressing room next door. She went in to his bedroom to quieten him, she said she was going to try to persuade him to go to sleep. She was in there quite a while. At last she made some excuse and came out. I could hardly contain myself outside the door. I kept wondering what that old man was forcing her to do . . . She was in her slip, half naked when she came out . . . I grabbed hold of her. I was half crazy, I could have strangled her! But she pressed her mouth to mine, half to keep me quiet, she twined herself round me and then, with that strange logic these girls have it struck her that it would calm me down if she gave herself to me . . . I took her there and then, on the carpet, with a kind of vile glee, thinking of the other one who had just pawed her and was next door waiting. It was a sort of hideous delight that you wouldn't understand. We never loved so fiercely. We must have rolled over onto the parquet floor, hit a piece of furniture. He got alarmed and suddenly there he was, gigantic—I'd never set eyes on him, he was a very tall man, naked, repugnant, holding a sword he'd taken down from the wall . . . So then I flung myself at him . . . (*He adds after a pause.*) The rest of it was her idea. It was only then that I discovered what it was she had to help him do every night . . . After we'd set the scene we left, taking nothing with us, or so I thought. But, out of bravado, or else to justify her absence from the house, she insisted on ending the evening in this casino, which was the nearest one . . . She pulled out of her suitcase a dance dress, covered in sequins, an unbelievable affair, the only thing she'd taken with her —it was so typical. She stripped naked in the car to put it on and we made love again on the back seat . . . And then we came on here to dance. She looked beautiful. She'd never looked so lovely as she did that night . . . And there was a sort of defiance to it, she wanted to flaunt herself with me in this hotel, where she knew my wife and my small daughter were upstairs asleep . . . And I agreed to it all, like a coward.

(*The* MUSICIANS *have come in, in dinner jackets and evening dresses. In the altered lighting, which has changed to red, they strike up an extravagant Thirties style tango. The* OLD TRAMP, *all diamonds and spangles, comes in dancing, her arms twined round the young man. She isn't quite the raddled hag she was in the first act; her body is young and slim in her marvellous dress but her makeup is strange; white and outrageously painted over the wrinkles, a death's head. They are alone on the dance floor. The entire establishment look at them, terrorstruck. They are "The Young Man and Death" of medieval engravings.*)

MAN. (*Strangely.*) It's horrible! He seems to be dancing with death.

SUPERINTENDENT. (*Quietly.*) He's dancing with insolence and beauty and youth just now. Your sight is bad. (*The* OLD WOMAN *is dancing, not with the ridiculous airs and graces of her first appearance, but with movements which are terrifying and full of a kind of grandeur, only her mask is nightmarish.*)

OLD WOMAN. We are handsome my darling, we're young. We've made love twice this evening—once on the floor of his house and once in the back of your car and we'll do it again soon in our room. We reek of love, the pair of us. Look at them, look at them all! They can smell it. They're sniffing it, uneasily, with their poor dreary bums glued with fright to their chairs, poor respectable bums, with the cheeks all tight. It's true you know, their bums are like their faces—all screwed up! It reeks of love in here since we've come in. It smells of fuck suddenly in their nice clean casino. It's chaos, it's misrule, it's Gomorrah! Look at them. Not one of them will dare to dance while we're on the floor. They're leaving us to dance alone, like kings, like pirates doomed to die! They feel they ought to call the police, or the manager or the head waiter—somebody who'll stop the scandal, but they don't dare. We're customers and they wouldn't want to do anything wrong. Besides my dress is by Schiaparelli, their silly fat wives have noticed that. And that's impressed them no matter what they say. It cost six month's rent from their tenant farmers, this dress. And it's mine. I earned it. Mine—like my little whore's breasts, like my behind that I'm wiggling under their noses. And I do what I like with it too. My laugh is mine. My joy is mine. I stink of love and they know I'm saying sod the lot of you. And the beauty of it is that under their hate and their contempt and their turmoil they're vaguely wondering whether they haven't all lived their lives like maggots. (*She cries out with savage laugh.*) That's the Revolution, Tigerpuss! But it makes you thirsty. (*She sinks down at a table, dragging him with her.*) Waiter! Champagne! And take two bottles to the band. Let's have a laugh, vagabonds all! It smells of mould in here. (*A moment of panic among the waiters and the reception staff who have come running in. They all confer, bumping into one another in their consternation. Eventually the champagne arrives. The hotel guests rise and start to go out, including the* GRANDMOTHER *who had come in with* ANNE MARIE, *older now and the* TWO CHILDREN.)

GRANDMOTHER. Let's go upstairs, Anne Marie! Come, children. This is no spectacle for you. I never thought this establishment could fall so low. (*The room is empty. Only the weird pair remain, sprawled at a table, a little breathless, and further upstage, the* MAN *who is watching them, fascinated, and the* SUPERINTENDENT.)

OLD WOMAN. (*With a sudden strange tenderness, taking the* YOUNG MAN's *hand.*) Say something . . . Are you a bit afraid still, darling? I'll teach you courage too. That's the secret of it all. The old bastard was born to it—one must say that for him. The old devil wasn't afraid of anything ever. Along with all the vices, he taught me that too. His pleasure right off as soon as the urge took him and he'd pay—with his money or his blood, depending. I can't tell you how many times I've brought him back to the house all battered with the fights he'd been in. My father was a huge bully of a man who terrorised the neighbourhood but in front of him he'd quake like a small boy. He was a nobleman from ancient times, one of the breed who'd conquered everything by force. He explained it all to me; the nobles, the real ones, had all been bandits once . . . (*She adds in a hard voice.*) Do you know, if he'd been thirty years younger I do think I could have loved the swine. (*The orchestra, after a short whispered consultation, has sent the two old* MUSICIANS *over to thank the* MAN *for the champagne. The* FIRST MUSICIAN *approaches the table, violin under his arm, champagne glass in hand.*)

MUSICIAN. Sir, madam, my colleagues in the orchestra have sent me to convey their thanks and if you would care to choose something you would like us to play for you, it would give us all very great pleasure to—

OLD WOMAN. (*Clinking glasses.*) All right old son, don't overdo it! Here's to you. Any old thing will do, but play it at the table.

OLD MUSICIAN. (*Slightly bothered.*) The trouble is, it's not quite the thing in this establishment. And I don't know that I can take it on myself to . . . Perhaps we ought to consult the management. . . .

OLD WOMAN. (*Superb.*) Management my arse. I'm not quite the thing in this establishment either. Play, I tell you! (*The* OLD MUSICIAN *darts a panicking look at his colleagues then starts to play a languorous gypsy number at the table. The* OLD WOMAN, *affected by the violin, says:*) I'll teach you life, my pet . . . I'll teach you love . . . (*She says confidentially.*) You know, even on the floor, or up against a wall, you can still feel tenderness—all the more so. That's another thing the other lot don't know. Adding two and two, that's all they know, silly sods! (*The* OLD VIOLINIST *plays. She listens a while and then says with a kind of tender complicity.*) You know that great heavy suitcase I struggled to carry down the drive . . . there was more inside than my grand dress and my three pairs of knickers . . . Those two big parcels wrapped in newspaper, that was gold . . . (*She gives a little laugh.*) Nobody knew he had it, it was hidden under the floorboards in his room. He didn't trust the men he did business with, the old fox, so he sent me along to buy it two years ago, from a bank over in Bordeaux, where nobody knew him. Nobody knew about it, only him and me.

YOUNG MAN. (*Dully.*) I don't want his gold.

OLD WOMAN. (*Softly.*) You won't ever see it, sweet. We'll use it to gamble with. And with it we'll win beautiful, brand new banknotes. Casino notes have no smell. It's lovely money that doesn't smell of sweat. And we'll spend them fast, on silly things—on nothing—just to shine, and have a laugh and watch their faces as we blue the precious stuff they all respect so much! (*She adds secretively.*) Besides, you know, I earned that gold. I earned it with my youth. I've never told you, but when he bought me from my father, the old bastard, I still longed for the moon—oh yes, I did! As much as for that white communion dress I never had. (*She cries with sudden violence to the* OLD MAN *who is still playing.*) Ah piss off you—or I'll start to howl in a minute! (*She straightens, giving her orders.*) Waiter. Go and tell the reception clerk, or the night porter if the silly sod's asleep, that we want a suite. Number seventeen, the most expensive in the house. The royal suite, they call it, because that's where they put Farouk that time he came here to treat his stinking lump of flesh, drunken old hog . . . (*She adds, superb and jaunty.*) Put your hand on my behind as we go up, Tigerpuss, let them all know what we're going to do. They'll get one more attack of the gripes and good luck to them. It's a wonder they don't burst, the way they eat. (*They make a triumphant exit, under the thunderstruck gaze of the entire hotel lounge. The* HALL PORTER *rushes up, outraged.*)

PORTER. I beg your pardon, ladies and gentlemen,

Chief Superintendent, I beg your pardon! The previous management would never have tolerated such a thing, never! But that young person spends a great deal of money here and her protector holds the majority of the shares in the Farming Cooperative. So one puts up with it. One puts up with everything! The hotel business isn't what it was! (*He goes out with a great despairing gesture, as if he were off to hang himself. The* MUSICIANS *clink glasses in the now empty lounge.*)

MUSICIANS.

Here's to you!

Mud in your eye, old thing!

Chin chin!

She's got spunk, that girl. Did you see the way she bawled them out? No skin off her nose. She's the girl friend of the chief shareholder!

Even so . . . it takes some nerve.

MOTHER. (*With a sudden cry.*) Alberto, where's Alberto?

MUSICIANS.

Here we go!

They're always looking for each other, those two.

Alberto—what are you on about? He was here a minute ago.

No he wasn't. He didn't come back after the interval, you're right!

OLD MUSICIAN. Hell, we've played two numbers, and never noticed we hadn't got a sax! Very weird thing, is music.

MOTHER. He said he was going to the lavatory. Oh, my God, he's still in there! (*She rushes wildly out, followed by one of the* MUSICIANS.)

MUSICIANS.

He's probably got gutsache.

Or he's jammed the bolt. That happened to me once when I was a child.

He'd have called for help. He's not a child now.

Perhaps he was taken queer?

Don't you believe it. He's in a mood. I think they had another row, him and her, over the kid.

(*The* MOTHER *and the* MUSICIAN *enter carrying the body of* ALBERTO. *The* LITTLE BOY *and the* LITTLE GIRL *run in, hand in hand, and look on, silently.*)

MOTHER. (*Braying.*) A doctor! Fetch a doctor! (*The* MUSICIANS *bustle about, bumping into each other.*)

MUSICIANS.

Lay him flat!

What a business!

God, he's heavy!

The customers shouldn't be seeing this!

He's white as chalk!

It can't be a stroke, not at his age!

Get some arnica!

Smelling salts!

Iodine!

There's aspirin in my bag!

He's coming round. He's trying to say something!

ALBERTO. (*Faintly.*) The pernod . . .

MOTHER. (*Holding him up.*) What about the pernod, my grizzly bear?

ALBERTO. The Pernod was poisoned . . . (*He falls back inert.*)

MUSICIAN. (*Feeling his pulse.*) Dead.

GIRL. (*Murmuring.*) Lord. Nice for the band that is.

MOTHER. (*Hurling herself on top of him, yelling.*) My great dog, my wolf! It's me, your love, your tart, your doxy! Speak to me! Speak to me! Say something!

MUSICIAN. (*Inanely.*) Like what? (*The light has dimmed on this harrowing scene. The* MUSICIANS *carry the body discreetly away in the gloom.*)

SUPERINTENDENT. (*To the* MAN.) And did he say something?

MAN. (*With a smile.*) No.

SUPERINTENDENT. (*Cheerfully.*) Pity. It might have been interesting. (*The lights fade to blackout during this brief interchange. They come up again immediately, full and real, with the orchestra up on its stand, playing a very lively piece, and* ALBERTO, *in excellent health, blowing away on his saxophone. The* LITTLE BOY *and the* LITTLE GIRL *are no longer there. The* MAN *and the* SUPERINTENDENT *have not moved. The* SUPERINTENDENT *asks:*) It wasn't true, of course?

MAN. (*With another strange smile.*) No. The kitchen hand hadn't put anything in his glass . . . But the lad had dreamed of it so much . . . (*He adds, harder.*) He couldn't bear the men who touched his mother.

SUPERINTENDENT. (*Incisive, suddenly.*) Nor the men who touched the woman he loved, later on? —and the two things merged somewhat?

MAN. (*Dully.*) Yes.

SUPERINTENDENT. He should have thought of that during the trial. It's so easy with a good counsel, to hint at emotional provocation. And come the reckoning it doesn't cost so much.

MAN. He wouldn't hear of it. He had a kind of honesty.

SUPERINTENDENT. Yes. They talk about vices and in the end, it's always honesty that trips you up. Very amusing creatures, men. (*He sees the* YOUNG MAN *come in. He says with sudden hardness.*) Now to business. (*He moves to the* YOUNG MAN *who has taken his raincoat from the stand and is about to leave.*) Frederick Walter?

YOUNG MAN. (*Surprised.*) Yes?

SUPERINTENDENT. (*Showing his card.*) Chief Superintendent Javron of the Surete. I have a warrant for your arrest. But while we're waiting for transport, we may as well begin. (*He draws him over to the table.*) Sit down. You are accused of the murder of the Vicomte de Lepaud. I must warn you that what you are about to say may be used in evidence, and that you may refuse to speak without the presence of your advocate.

YOUNG MAN. I don't want an advocate.

MAN. (*Drawing near, with a kind of diffidence.*) Not even me?

YOUNG MAN. Are you a lawyer? (*The* MAN *does not answer. The* THREE MEN *are all seated.*)

SUPERINTENDENT. (*To the approaching* WAITER.) Would you ask the band to stop playing? (*The* WAITER *goes to talk to the band, who stop playing, and comes back.*)

WAITER. The musicians would like to know if they may leave?

SUPERINTENDENT. No. They may be asked to give evidence. Nobody is to move from the Casino. We shall probably be needing everyone. (*The* WAITER *moves away. The* SUPERINTENDENT *turns to the* YOUNG MAN *and goes into the attack.*) Your name is Frederick Walter. You are twenty seven years old. You were born on the 27th of June 1919 at Montluçon, to Lucien Walter, tailor, and his wife Germaine, née Couture, musician. On his return from the War, your father was unable to restart his business in this town and he moved to Paris to work at his trade of tailor cutter. You went through normal schooling and then entered Technical College from which you were dismissed at the end of your first year. You then worked at a variety of jobs, without any great success, until the day when you met and married a childhood sweetheart Anne Marie Delafont, whose mother gave you a managerial post in her factory. You had two children of this marriage and you left your wife for Maria Josepha Percepied, of no specific profession, but who styled herself housekeeper to the Vicomte de Lepaud, being at the time in residence at the latter's ancestral domicile. Are these facts correct?

YOUNG MAN. Yes.

SUPERINTENDENT. On the 28th of September 1947 the Vicomte de Lepaud was found strangled, hanged with a silk scarf from the hasp of one of the windows in his bedroom. The girl Maria Josepha Percepied had left the chateau that very evening, weary, so she said, of her protector's shabby treatment of her. In actual fact, it was to go to you. The night of the murder your presence was made known in this establishment where you both danced and swilled champagne before taking a room, where you stayed for the following day and night.

YOUNG MAN. Yes.

SUPERINTENDENT. In running away with her as you did and leaving your job at you mother-in-law's factory, what means of support did you have in mind for both of you?

YOUNG MAN. (*With an isolent smile.*) Did you ever run off with a girl you were madly in love with?

SUPERINTENDENT. (*A bit put out.*) No. I've led a very simple family life.

YOUNG MAN. Pity. It would have saved you asking the question.

SUPERINTENDENT. (*Slightly nettled.*) Admittedly

you weren't without funds to pay for your wild goings on in the early days. But you spent a great deal . . . all the evidence points to that. After that, what did you live on?

YOUNG MAN. Gambling.

SUPERINTENDENT. You lost some very big sums quite often.

YOUNG MAN. Yes we did. Our winnings of the previous night.

SUPERINTENDENT. Did you know the vicomte de Lepaud?

YOUNG MAN. No.

SUPERINTENDENT. Your mother had spent her entire youth in these parts. You even lived here yourself up until you were four. Had you never heard talk of him?

YOUNG MAN. Of course—who hadn't?

SUPERINTENDENT. Before that night when you came to the lime walk to wait for Mlle Percepied, had you never been to the place?

YOUNG MAN. Yes. As a child. Like a lot of local boys.

SUPERINTENDENT. In what circumstances?

YOUNG MAN. All the village children used to climb the wall to raid the orchards or find birds nests.

SUPERINTENDENT. But to the house itself? With your mother? We have evidence to that effect from an old manservant of the Viscount's.

YOUNG MAN. (*A pause.*) I was four. Five maybe. I've forgotten.

SUPERINTENDENT. A visit to this mysterious place, to see this notorious man whose scandalous life had the whole locality by the ears—that should have left you with some sort of memory though, shouldn't it?

YOUNG MAN. No.

SUPERINTENDENT. Let's leave that . . . After that

visit, which you don't remember, you never saw the viscount again?

YOUNG MAN. Never. Why should I have? I moved to Paris with my family.

SUPERINTENDENT. Your mother, when she started playing in orchestras, did several seasons here in this casino, which is only some fifty kilometres from the Lepaud residence.

YOUNG MAN. I had no reason to go back there. I was a small boy on holiday and my bicycle rides didn't take me very far afield. I didn't settle in the neighbourhood until my marriage with Anne Marie Delafont.

SUPERINTENDENT. And the Delafont family weren't on visiting terms with the Viscount?

YOUNG MAN. (*With a smile.*) You can't know the local customs very well. There was an unbridgeable gulf between the Delafonts, who were rich business people of ordinary middle class origin and the lord at the Big House. Old Mother Delafont, even in her wildest moments of vainglory, never dreamed she could ever cross the threshold.

SUPERINTENDENT. And yet—if one's to believe that old manservant of the Viscount's—your mother did cross it.

YOUNG MAN. The vicomte de Lepaud used sometimes to ask the taximan who drove him home to share a bottle, if the man amused him—but never the local notables. With the taximan the social difference was so great as to be virtually invisible. But he would have thought it totally absurd to offer a cup of tea to the wife of the Presiding Magistrate.

SUPERINTENDENT. (*With a faint smile, eyeing him.*) You seem to understand him rather well. You talk about him with a certain sympathy . . .

YOUNG MAN. (*Evasively.*) Perhaps. With time . . .

SUPERINTENDENT. At the Casino, as a small boy, as the pianist's son, you mixed with the children of the hotel guests. That was a somewhat awkward position and perhaps humiliating too, at times. Did you suffer from it at all?

YOUNG MAN. I don't recall doing so, no.

SUPERINTENDENT. You didn't ever feel, given your intelligence and the quality of your personality, that you deserved better and that fate had been, to some extent, unfair?

YOUNG MAN. I don't know what you mean.

SUPERINTENDENT. (*Abruptly.*) Forgive me if this is hurtful to you but we have witnesses who all affirm that as a very young woman, either before or immediately after her marriage, your mother was the vicomte de Lepaud's mistress. Is this news to you?

YOUNG MAN. (*After a pause.*) No.

SUPERINTENDENT. You were a difficult child, touchy, secretive, uneasy in his own skin. Proud and sensitive to an unhealthy degree. What information we've been able to gather from your mother's musician friends and from your old playmates all stresses this point. Your mother had affairs with various men. This was a grief to you. During the 1929 summer season, here in this very casino, your mother formed an attachment to a member of the band, one Alberto Bachmann, a saxophonist. Now, nothing was ever established, I can tell you that right away—and besides, it pertains to the juvenile courts and couldn't be held against you now—but rumour has it that you tried repeatedly, with concoctions of your own making—all quite harmless as it happens—to do away with this man. Is that correct?

YOUNG MAN. Possibly. I don't remember. I've never had any childhood memories. Everything's a blank.

SUPERINTENDENT. Very convenient.

YOUNG MAN. You think so? It can be agonising. Lucky the man who can still walk hand in hand with the untroubled little boy that he once was. My childhood is a fog with very few faces showing through.

SUPERINTENDENT. Your mother's among them, though, surely?

YOUNG MAN. (*Dully.*) I loved her passionately, as a child. Then as I got older, I grew to hate her. It's only since she died, that a picture of the carefree, loving young woman that she must have been emerges for me. Her scent, on the pillow that I used to hug at night before I went to sleep—something else I'd forgotten—has come back to me, like an absolution.

MAN. (*Suddenly.*) Your mother loved you. That I can tell you.

YOUNG MAN. (*Aggressively.*) What do you know about it?

MAN. (*Dully.*) I knew her too.

SUPERINTENDENT. And out of that childhood fog, what other images emerge?

YOUNG MAN. Faces of a few musicians in the band, a few members of the hotel staff. The face of an old night porter, in particular, whom I was very fond of and who must be dead by now.

SUPERINTENDENT. No. We found him. We'll question him in due course. The face of Alberto Bachmann?

YOUNG MAN. Yes. I haven't forgotten that one. Is he still alive?

SUPERINTENDENT. Yes. He'll give his evidence too. Among your memories, dim as they may be, what image do you have of the vicomte de Lepaud?

YOUNG MAN. (*Harshly, after a pause.*) An old man, naked, repugnant, with a sword in his hand, looking at me and cackling.

MAN. (*Half rising.*) Don't, boy!

SUPERINTENDENT. (*Pushing him gently down in his seat.*) You can advise him later, but you can't interrupt this preliminary hearing. I asked him a question and he replied of his own free will. (*He goes on after a pause.*) Hasn't the Vicomte some other face for you, younger, more affectionate maybe? A face from the last visit just before you both left the neighbourhood —you and your mother?

YOUNG MAN. (*Dully.*) Not more affectionate, no. Curious. He eyed me with a kind of malevolent irony. He murmured with a disdainful curl of his lip, 'He looks like a girl.' Then he added with a playful touch of his fist to my chin, 'He's got my jaw though. He'll be a tiger. Take good care of him. We'll see what we can do for him later on.'

SUPERINTENDENT. Did your mother say anything to you after that visit?

YOUNG MAN. No. I just remember that she told my father a lie when we got home. She said we'd been to say goodbye to the headmaster of my school. And when I told my inquisitive aunts that we'd been to see a gentleman at the big house, they all tittered and made faces. We left for Paris the next day.

SUPERINTENDENT. And your mother never said anything to you?

YOUNG MAN. (*Dully, after a pause.*) Much later she did, yes. When I was ten or so. I'd been told off by the hotel manager one gala evening—and sent out of the ballroom—where a child has no business to be, I know— She told me I was the son of a prince and I had to be prouder than the others, who were nothing compared to me.

SUPERINTENDENT. And what did that revelation do to you?

YOUNG MAN. It helped me to feel different. And even more alone.

SUPERINTENDENT. And during the whole of your childhood you never saw the vicomte de Lepaud again?

YOUNG MAN. (*Harshly.*) No. He was never curious enough to want to see me.

MAN. (*Suddenly.*) Yes. Once. When you were twenty. You aren't telling it all. Now you have to. At your mother's funeral. He came. Why I wonder? If he'd had to bury all the girls he'd known . . . There was no hunting that day, I expect. He shook your hand, with that amused smile of his, and that enquiring little glint in his eye as he studied you. You stood and faced each other for some seconds, with the winter wind lifting the women's veils and the whole village in black around you watching, and the priest who had stopped praying. Because of course everybody knew. The whole village had long ago recognized that lordly jawbone.

SUPERINTENDENT. And what did you feel during this brief confrontation with the man who had given you life?

YOUNG MAN. (*Simply.*) Hatred.

SUPERINTENDENT. Later on, did he recognise you, when he burst in, sword in hand, into that dark little dressing room where you were tumbling that girl?

YOUNG MAN. Yes. He knew me.

SUPERINTENDENT. Did he say anything?

YOUNG MAN. He said 'Little bastard' and he hurled himself onto me. (*Stagehands have come in and start shifting the furniture and sending the decor up into the flies.*)

SUPERINTENDENT. (*Irritably.*) What's going on? I said we weren't to be disturbed!

MAN. (*Neutrally.*) They're setting up the cathedral scene. That's where the whole thing has to end.

SUPERINTENDENT. Let them be quiet about it then. (*During the ensuing scenes the set gradually changes until the Cathedral appears.*) Frederick Walter, you have just confessed to strangling the vicomte de Lepaud. Did you strangle him to get the girl you wanted—the girl he had, let us admit it, defiled—or to get your revenge on him for creating you and then abandoning you to a world where you were always to find yourself alone? (*The* YOUNG MAN *does not answer. The* SUPERINTENDENT *goes on quietly.*) I'm handing you a lifeline and the answer you give me may influence the jury's decision one way or the other. It's a case of saving your neck, Frederick Walter. Not that parricide—even adulterous, if I may so put it—is an extenuating circumstance in the eyes of the law. But still, although nothing has yet been proved, the implication of a crime for sordid personal gain will weigh on the minds of the jury and it is likely to weigh infinitely more heavily than hatred.

YOUNG MAN. (*Closed.*) All this finessing makes me sick. I've pleaded guilty. Your work is done.

MAN. (*Quietly.*) May I help him to answer?

SUPERINTENDENT. If you like.

MAN. When you saw him there suddenly, in front of you, in his repulsive nakedness, with his tigerish old mask of a face snarling—when he smashed his hand across your face with that irony and that icy contempt in his eyes that you knew so well, after he'd dragged the girl back by the wrist—who was it you saw suddenly in his grip?

YOUNG MAN. (*Dully.*) My mother. My mother as a small girl, in old photographs.

MAN. That degraded, half naked slut, cowed already

and submissive, and willing to be taken back by that depraved old male if you didn't kill him right away—that was her, wasn't it?

YOUNG MAN. Yes. (*A pause.*)

SUPERINTENDENT. (*Quietly.*) Whether or not he loved your mother—and that you'll never know—that man was still your father.

YOUNG MAN. (*Violently.*) No! My father was a tailor. He used to cut suits, gravely and calmly, standing at his bench. Then afterwards he'd explain gently to his workpeople how to do it or not to do it . . . From early morning he'd cut away with his big scissors that never made a mistake, working to keep us fed. And in the evening, when he came home, he'd lift me up in those big strong hands of his, that had worked away all day, and he'd look into my eyes and ask me if I'd been good, and not made mamma cry. And he had great sad eyes because Mother didn't love him. And young as I was, I used to lie to him so that he wouldn't be hurt. I never told him when she had gone out . . . He worked right through to the end, humbly, without asking anything from life but the love I gave him . . . And my mother, who was jealous, kept telling me that he was nothing to me, but it made no difference, I never had any other father. That night of the 28th of September, I set the record straight, that's all. (*A pause while the sceneshifters go on working silently around them. The* MAN *concludes, heavily.*)

MAN. He was a prince too.

YOUNG MAN. Yes. And I'm proud of him. (*The* MAN *rises and goes to him and takes his arm with awkward shyness.*)

MAN. I misjudged you, lad, I'm sorry. Forgive me.

YOUNG MAN. (*Looking at him, disquieted.*) Why do you say that? Who are you?

MAN. A traveller you met yesterday at the station, whose name you didn't even ask. A friend.

YOUNG MAN. (*Closed.*) I have no friends. I'm alone.

MAN. (*Gently.*) One never stops being alone, my little soldier. You hold your few yards of trench, firing alone into the night against an enemy whose face you'll never see, with the barrel of your gun burning your frozen fingers. It's an endless winter campaign with no way out of it but death. And it wouldn't be so bad if one knew what one was fighting for.

SUPERINTENDENT. (*Crisply.*) One day, it would seem, the losses seriously outweighed the winnings of the night before and you both realised that you hadn't any more money. You decided to rob a small bank in the vicinity. With the help of a stolen car, you held up the van that was delivering payroll funds, and you fired to cover your getaway, seriously wounding two men.

MAN. (*Straightening suddenly.*) Let him be now. From here on, you're dealing with me.

SUPERINTENDENT. (*Irked.*) Not yet. My colleagues will have that dirty job. I haven't retired yet and he's still my pigeon. That arrogant little pair with everything going for them—youth, beauty, luck—who gave half the country the jitters for six months! Did you ever see the film, when you broke jail—the one they made from your story? There's nothing some people won't turn into money. Two insolent little angels of pleasure and death. Oh, the film boys went to town. And all the morons in their slippers lapping it up over their supper, gawping at the television as they bashed their kids! Tell me, was it as good for you in real life as it was on the films?

YOUNG MAN. (*Dully.*) No. She started running around. She met someone—a man who'd helped us do a job. A fellow who was nearer her sort than I was, and she gave herself to him.

(*Gradually all the characters in the play have appeared in the dimly lit set. The* MUSICIANS *have come down from their platform, which is swiftly removed by the sceneshifters. They form into a huddle a little way upstage, like spectators at a trial, and listen.* MARIA JOSEPHA, *young as she was earlier, in the Cathedral, but in her lovely spangled evening dress, leaves the group and comes forward.*)

MARIA JOSEPHA. Oh, Tigerpuss, you always use such big words. You don't understand anything about anything. You may have brought off all your big jobs like a king of the toughs and shot it out like a hero with the fuzz, but you'll always be a prissypants. I ask you, what does it mean 'gave herself to him'? To Old Marcel? A petty crook like him with his ugly little mug?

YOUNG MAN. Didn't you sleep with him?

MARIA JOSEPHA. Of course I slept with him. For a month if you want to know. But you don't have to talk like a chained bible! Gave myself to him! Whatever next? I never gave myself to anybody except myself. Nor has anybody. Nor have you.

YOUNG MAN. (*With a cry.*) Me?

MARIA JOSEPHA. (*Chanting with an amiable giggle.*) 'I left everything for you. My daughter and my native land!' Do you remember that great beanpole warbling that in 'Salome,' that time we went to see the touring company at the Casino? What a laugh she gave us though . . . ! (*She cries suddenly, harsh and vulgar.*) Left everything my eye. And why? Because she'd taken a mighty big fancy to the young feller, right? Oh, sure— Love. Love of herself. We all do that. Nobody gives anything. Try to be honest with yourself for once, little snotface. (*The* MAN *goes to her and takes her by the arm with a kind of firm affectionate familiarity and turns her to face him.*)

MAN. Are you sure you never gave anything, you little fool? That night when you collapsed into my arms, sobbing with fear, with that great heavy suitcase—what did you say to me, with your face buried in my neck? (MARIA JOSEPHA *looks at him astounded, then exclaims comically.*)

MARIA JOSEPHA. My! —haven't you aged? I like the beard though, it suits you. (*They look at each other. She falters a little under his gaze and admits reluctantly.*) Yes . . . I did love you . . . At least I think I did . . . Or I would have done if I'd had nothing else to do, like the girls in the class you come from . . . But we didn't have much time to go into our emotions, with the life we led. Do you remember? It only lasted six months but it was still worth it, wasn't it? (*A youthful smile crosses the* MAN*'s face.*)

MAN. Yes.

MARIA JOSEPHA. (*With childish pride.*) Bonnie and Clyde. Do you remember how we read about them in the papers at the time? And we did almost as well as they did, considering we weren't American . . . The flurry and scurry there was for six whole months—the panic! We popped up everywhere. We succeeded everytime. Oh we had our money's worth all right! Do you regret it?

MAN. (*With amused tenderness.*) No.

MARIA JOSEPHA. Nobles we were. Real ones, like those in the olden days that the old man used to talk about. (*She cries out wildly.*) Yes, you fool, I loved you, but you didn't even notice! (*She adds stonily.*) Besides you were always thinking about your wife and kids and I've never forgiven you for that.

SUPERINTENDENT. Are Anne Marie Delafont and the children there? (*The* YOUNG WOMAN, *looking as she did in the Cathedral scene, leaves the group and steps forward with the* CHILDREN. *The* SUPERINTENDENT *thumbs through his papers.*) Are you Anne Marie Delafont (born 17th September 1921 at Gueret, to Francois Gastom Delafont and his wife Gabrielle)—divorced spouse of Frederick Walter?

YOUNG WOMAN. (*Distinctly.*) No. I'm still his wife. I never sued for divorce.

SUPERINTENDENT. (*Grumbling as he goes through his papers.*) Are you sure? What have they given me here? They've put you down as divorced, decree absolute granted on the—

YOUNG WOMAN. There must have been some confusion. I asked for a legal separation—I needed the power to sign papers for the children's schooling and such . . . But I never asked for a divorce.

SUPERINTENDENT. (*In his papers.*) That must be it then. You pay people to do a job and they never do it properly. So, you never wanted a divorce, you say?

YOUNG WOMAN. No.

SUPERINTENDENT. Why not? You had all possible grounds for one.

YOUNG WOMAN. I was his wife. (*The* MAN *and the* YOUNG WOMAN *are face to face, the* YOUNG WOMAN *says in a hard voice.*) And I meant it to be for life.

MAN. One nice young man, paid for cash down, with good Delafont money, right? Property's property! We know our rights, don't we?

YOUNG WOMAN. (*More gently.*) You're not being fair.

MAN. I was choking to death living with you.

YOUNG WOMAN. Maybe so, but I was your wife.

MAN. Because we signed a register? My kind—events taught you that—don't pay too much attention to signatures.

YOUNG WOMAN. Not just because we signed the register.

MAN. Because we said it in church to that old man in fancy dress who tore through the service like an overworked clerk, because he still had a funeral to do before he could have his lunch?

YOUNG WOMAN. It wasn't him we said it to.

MAN. To God, perhaps? There's always a perhaps with that one.

YOUNG WOMAN. Your religious education was always a bit shaky, my poor man, I know that. But mine was sound, and I told you at the time. Marriage is a free sacrament. Nobody was ever married against his will. The vows you make are to yourself. God is only the witness.

MAN. (*Unpleasantly.*) And suppose one morning the tender girl of the night before turns into a little bookkeeper, certain of her rights, just like her mother and her grandmother and all the other moneyed women of the tribe? What if one starts to wonder what one's doing in all this?

YOUNG WOMAN. (*Quietly.*) She's still your wife, because you wanted it that way. You should have thought of all that at the time.

MAN. (*With a mirthless laugh.*) You've got it all worked out, haven't you? When you make a contract, Lord help us all. (*He looks at her again.*) I was never one of your breed. Nor that old vulture's either, who sired me by accident, one lecherous night. And I didn't belong in that poor tawdry gang of wretches in the orchestra. And one has to belong somewhere. (*To the* SUPERINTENDENT *violently.*) That's it. We've done enough talking. Words turn my stomach. I am Frederick Walter. I confess to everything, and I can tell you a lot more besides. There's nothing I haven't done —But now that's it, finish! I'm entitled to a bit of peace. Pull me in now and shove me in a cell where I can be alone. Anyway it won't change anything much. (*He holds out his wrists as he did in the earlier scene. The* SUPERINTENDENT *remains with his hands in his pockets, smiling.*)

SUPERINTENDENT. I told you before, I haven't any handcuffs, Frederick Walter. And we're not concerned with any of that now.

MAN. I tell you I want to be alone.

SUPERINTENDENT. (*Quietly.*) You are. With a few extras in the background, just as everybody else has. Look around you, at all the characters in your life. There are a few false friends missing, a few forgotten girls, but it's a full house, near enough. (*The* MAN *looks at them all, distraught. He catches sight of his tall rather ungainly daughter and asks brusquely.*)

MAN. You're the girl, are you?

DAUGHTER. Yes.

MAN. (*Searching his memory.*) Marie Christine?

DAUGHTER. Yes.

MAN. Painted and powdered already, like a wellbred little tart?

DAUGHTER. (*Hard-voiced.*) You saw me last when I was sixteen and that was by chance.

MAN. That little warm wriggling thing who crawled over me in the evenings and rubbed herself against me like an enormous kitten—was that you?

DAUGHTER. Yes.

MAN. (*With an imperceptible breach in his hard-*

ness.) Yours were the eyes of love. The only ones, I do believe. And when I looked into your eyes as they gazed at me when you were three or four, I had faith almost, and acceptance. Show me, show me your eyes.

DAUGHTER. (*She looks at him calmly as he gazes at her anguished and says simply.*) I've grown up. (*He turns with a kind of apprehension to the* BOY.)

MAN. (*Roughly.*) What name did she give you?

BOY. What's that to you?

MAN. (*Murmuring.*) You were born after I left and I don't even know your name. (*A pause. He brushes the* BOY's *chin with his knuckles and says with his cold smile.*) He looks like a girl. He's got my jaw though. (*He cries suddenly distraught.*) Do we just go on, repeating the same pattern?

SUPERINTENDENT. I'm afraid so. (*The* MAN *casts a hunted look around him and cries suddenly, turning up his coat collar.*) What the hell are we doing in this deserted church? It's cold. (*Quietly.*) You're bound to feel a bit cold, Frederick Walter and there's nothing to be done about that. You're dead, and you're reliving that one little second of eternity I was telling you about . . . Do you remember? The tiny second when the heart has stopped and the blood flows one last time through the brain, if my modest theory is correct. (*The* MAN *looks at him. He goes on.*) At this moment, you are lying by the ditch, on the route nationale 84. A few yards away your car—what's left of it—is burning against a pylon. You crashed while making a getaway—your last. The cops caught up with you, vaguely relieved, and bothered at the same time—death is always a bothersome thing. They're doing their best to cover your mangled body with a blanket and the last real thing you'll ever see is the sight of their two stupid, worried faces bending over you. . . . A little potted version of the significance of life, you might say . . . We are only images in your last memory. (*The* MAN *remains dumbstruck in the middle of the stage, while the others look on, embarrassed. Suddenly he asks like a child.*)

MAN. What do I have to do? Should I lie down? I don't know what one's supposed to do, quite . . .

SUPERINTENDENT. (*At a loss too.*) I don't either. Perhaps you should lie down I think, yes . . .

MAN. (*He hesitates, awkward and touching. He catches sight of the* LITTLE BOY *and calls:*) Hey, boy! (*The* CHILD *approaches. The* MAN *takes his arm, then takes the* YOUNG MAN'S *too.*) And you too, my big lad. There might just be time to settle his hash if we all put our mind to it. I should enjoy that before I went.

LITTLE BOY. Shall we put something in his drink?

MAN. (*With a smile.*) No. That never comes off, that little ploy of yours. Our bare hands. They'll do. (*He consults the* YOUNG MAN, *conspiratorially.*) Won't they, lad, what do you say? (*He looks at him with a smile and says, with sudden gravity.*) I know I've bawled at you, called you a little libertine, a brute, an egoist . . . But you were so unhappy, you were searching for something too. We all are. And when we find it . . . (*He stops and brushes back the* YOUNG MAN'S *lock of hair.*) That hair of yours. . . . You'd never get it cut, would you? Funny, you're like my grownup son, now . . . (*The* LITTLE BOY *who has been upstage, comes back.*)

LITTLE BOY. He's coming. We made too much noise. He must have heard us.

MAN. (*A boy again with his mates.*) Look out, you lot! Let's not miss him this time! (*To the* BOY.) You do a dive and grab his legs. Big fellow here pins his arms behind his back.

LITTLE BOY. *I* want to strangle him! Why can't it be *me?* I'm the one it hurt the most!

MAN. No. You're too young. I'll take care of that. And we mustn't botch it this time. Let him come in a little way and then go for his legs. (*They wait, tense and still. The* MAN *asks the* BOY.) Not afraid, child, are you?

LITTLE BOY. No. (*More waiting. Then the* MAN *murmurs.*)

MAN. What the hell is he doing? Make a noise so he'll come out. Knock a chair onto the paving stones. (*The* BOY *knocks over a chair which echoes strangely on the stone floor of the Cathedral. The* MAN *listens.*) Look out! (*A step is heard on the flagstones, echoing in the vaulted roof. The Vicomte de* LEPAUD *surges out, naked, holding a sword. In point of fact it is a Samurai sword and the man is* ALBERTO BACHMANN, *holding a grimacing Japanese mask in front of his face, but one does not realise this immediately.*)

VICOMTE LEPAUD. What's going on? Who's there? (*All three hurl themselves onto him and hold him down. The* MAN *makes to strangle him. A short struggle.* BACHMANN *loses his mask and sword.*)

ALBERTO. (*Yelling.*) What do you think you're doing? Are you crazy? I got these things off the wall of the pub. It was just a laugh. Let me put my pants on will you? I'm in the raw. What's the matter with you —pack of savages you are! I was with my fancy bit, wasn't I? Can't a man have a bit of loving? She's a consenting adult. Let go my legs, you dirty little sod! Ow! (*To the* MAN.) Chief! Get him off me! The little swine's biting my leg!

MAN. Let him go.

ALBERTO. (*Rubbing his leg.*) You're a grown man, you are. Dammit we aren't kids. No need to make a song and dance about it. A bit of skirt's a bit of skirt, and that's as far as it goes. And hell! I'm not such a bad sort. I never hurt the lad. And considering all the filthy concoctions the little perisher got me to drink, I'd have had every right to. I was quite fond of the kid at first . . . Why I even taught him to blow on my saxophone, one night when he didn't have it in for me too much . . .

MAN. (*To the* YOUNG MAN *who is still holding him.*) Let him go.

ALBERTO. (*Shouting to the* MOTHER.) Hand me my dressing gown, you! Don't just stand there like a stuffed turnip! Fine nit I look without a stitch on! (*The* MOTHER *fusses round him, humbly, soothing him and helping him to dress.*)

MOTHER. There, there, my great woolly bear.

MAN. (*He looks at them, at a loss for words. At last he says:*) Poor bastard . . . It wears one out, trying to understand. And in the end, one understands it all. Perhaps that's why one feels so terribly tired.

SUPERINTENDENT. (*Who has been watching all this.*) I think maybe you ought to lie down . . .

MAN. (*Looking round helplessly.*) Where? There's nothing in this benighted church.

SUPERINTENDENT. (*To the others.*) Arrange some chairs for him. He'll be more comfortable. (*The others bring chairs and make a bed for him to lie on.*)

MAN. (*Lying down and asking uncertainly.*) I'd better lie down then, had I? I used to hate doing that, I hated going to bed. I was afraid I'd fall asleep before she came in . . . (*He asks anxiously, curled up on the chairs like a child.*) Is the orchestra still playing on the bandstand outside? (*The* MOTHER *comes forward and says gently, with a little stroke to his brow.*)

MOTHER. No. The music's over now. You can go to sleep. I'm back.

MAN. (*He looks at the* YOUNG WOMAN *leaning over him smiling and murmurs, a little embarrassed.*) Mother . . . why it's absurd . . . I'm older than you are. I've got grey hair . . .

MOTHER. (*Soothingly.*) No you haven't . . . What nonsense you're talking. Why you're burning hot. You're delirious . . . You're a little boy still, I'm back now and you can go to sleep . . . I shan't leave the room tonight. . . .

MAN. (*With a sigh of relief.*) That's good . . . (*He says suddenly, in the hurt voice of a little boy.*) Why did the manager send me out?

MOTHER. (*Gently.*) Because he's a coarse vulgar man. But you have to be prouder than they are. You're the son of a prince. (*The* MUSICIANS *have gathered round him. The old* NIGHT PORTER, *who appeared at the beginning of the play, emerges from their midst, crouches beside him and says kindly:*)

NIGHT PORTER. You know, lad, you mustn't be ashamed about being with musicians. Musicians are artists . . . They may look a bit trashy, but they're artists all the same. They aren't just out to make money like the rest . . . Take the manager, he thinks he's a gent, but he's only a mangy old lemonade peddlar. And with the Casino customers—same thing. All mangy peddlars of something. The musicians don't peddle anything but wind. They scrape away at their strings, they blow into their little pipes and they shift air, that's what they do. That's music . . . They're princes too . . . I've always thought the world of musicians. I'd love to have studied music if I'd had the wherewithal . . .

MAN. (*Smiling and at peace now.*) Yes. You always used to tell me that to comfort me, when I crept down at night to see you . . . (*He asks suddenly.*) Are you there, boy?

BOY. (*Coming forward.*) Yes.

MAN. Hold my hand. (*He suddenly stares fixedly at something. The* LITTLE GIRL *from the Cathedral scene emerges from the crowd, smiling, and says gently:*)

LITTLE GIRL. I'm here too. And I love you. We'll never be lonely again when we're married. (*The* MAN *smiles sadly, as if he knew it all, then gives a peaceful sigh.*)

MAN. No, we'll never be lonely again . . . (*Then in a different, calm tone he adds.*) We make a whole heavy chore of it and yet, it's so easy . . .

SUPERINTENDENT. (*Softly.*) Of course it's easy. It's like everything else. All you have to do is say yes. (*The* MAN *has closed his eyes. In the distance, one hears the eerie sound of an ambulance siren approaching along a country road. A fairly long pause, while they all look at him without daring to move, then one of the orchestra girls murmurs to her friend.*)

GIRL. Gawd, not a very cheerful ending, is it?

2ND GIRL. No, but it's lovely though . . . Anyway, it isn't true. It's only a story. It's never like that in real life. (*The curtain falls slowly on the motionless group.*)

THE END

THE SEA HORSE

EDWARD J. MOORE

(Little Theatre) Drama

I Man, I Woman, Interior

It is a play that is, by turns, tender, ribald, funny and suspenseful. Audiences everywhere will take it to their hearts because it is touched with humanity and illuminates with glowing sympathy the complexities of a man-woman relationship. Set in a West Coast waterfront bar, the play is about Harry Bales, a seaman, who, when on shore leave, usually heads for "The Sea Horse," the bar run by Gertrude Blum, the heavy, unsentimental proprietor. Their relationship is purely physical and, as the play begins, they have never confided their private yearnings to each other. But this time Harry has returned with a dream: to buy a charter fishing boat and to have a son by Gertrude. She, in her turn, has made her life one of hard work, by day, and nocturnal love-making; she has encased her heart behind a facade of toughness, utterly devoid of sentimentality, because of a failed marriage. Irwin's play consists in the ritual of "dance" courtship by Harry of Gertrude, as these two outwardly abrasive characters fight, make up, fight again, spin dreams, deflate them, make love and reveal their long locked-up secrets.

"A burst of brilliance!"—*N.Y. Post.* "I was touched close to tears!"—*Village Voice.* "A must! An incredible love story. A beautiful play!"—*Newhouse Newspapers.* "A major new playwright!"—*Variety.*

ROYALTY, $50–$35

THE AU PAIR MAN

HUGH LEONARD

(Little Theatre) Comedy

I Man, I Woman, Interior

The play concerns a rough Irish bill collector named Hartigan, who becomes a love slave and companion to an English lady named Elizabeth, who lives in a cluttered London town house, which looks more like a museum for a British Empire on which the sun has long set. Even the door bell chimes out the national anthem. Hartigan is immediately conscripted into her service in return for which she agrees to teach him how to be a gentleman rather after the fashion of a reverse Pygmalion. The play is a wild one, and is really the neverending battle between England and Ireland. Produced to critical acclaim at Lincoln Center's Vivian Beaumont Theatre.

ROYALTY, $50–$35